Milton for the Methodists

Milton for the Methodists

Emphasized extracts from
Paradise Lost
selected, edited, and annotated by
JOHN WESLEY

With an Introduction by Frank Baker

Epworth Press

British Library Cataloguing in Publication Data

Milton, John, *1608–1674*
Milton for the Methodists: emphasised
extracts from Paradise Lost.
1. Poetry in English. Milton, John
1608–1674, Paradise Lost—Critical
studies
I. Title   II. Wesley, John *1703–1791*
821'.4

ISBN 0–7162–0447–9

First published 1988 by
Epworth Press
Room 195, 1 Central Buildings
Westminster, London SW1H 9NR

Typeset by Input Typesetting Ltd, London
and printed in Great Britain by
Richard Clay Ltd, Bungay, Suffolk

Contents

Introduction

One of the most formative influences on the thought and writings of John and Charles Wesley was John Milton, and by way of return John Wesley in particular greatly helped in fostering the appreciation of Milton during the eighteenth century. Although it is likely that Milton's *Paradise Lost* formed a part of his family background, the story may well be apocryphal that when as a teenage scholar at the Charterhouse School in London the usher challenged Jacky about consorting mainly with younger boys, he replied, 'Better to rule in hell than to serve in heaven' – a slight variant of Satan's words in *Paradise Lost*, I.263.[1]

It seems that Wesley's own close study of Milton actually started after he had graduated at Oxford in 1724. Early in 1725 he began his lifelong diary, and inside the first opening wrote 'transcribed notes on Milton'; on 3 June he 'learned the geography of the First Book of Milton', and on 1 August began to 'collect' Milton, i.e. to prepare a precis, with consecutive extracts. On 19 September he noted his ordination as deacon by the Bishop of Oxford, and in the following September the purchase of his own copy of Milton. His ordination was a necessary step to scholarly promotion, and after the academic bustle of qualifying for his master's degree and securing election as a fellow of Lincoln College he did in fact spend three years as his father's curate at Wroot.

Recalled in November 1729 by the Rector of Lincoln College to service as a tutor, in 1730 Wesley returned with renewed enthusiasm to *Paradise Lost*. His diary shows that during 9–21 February and 2–11 March 1730, he prepared poetical and explanatory notes on Milton, and in May began to use them with his pupils; in June he worked on 'three books of Milton', and a further two in July.[2]

When he set out as a missionary to Georgia in October 1735 he took Milton with him. On 17 October 1736, he began a reading course of *Paradise Lost* with Mark Hird, and also with Sophy Hopkey, though in the case of that marriageable young woman he noted: 'But I expressly desired we might leave out the love parts of that poem, because (I said) they might hurt her mind.'[3] While travelling on foot in South Carolina towards the end of the following April he read *Paradise Regained*.

After his return to England and his spiritual transformation, Wesley was concerned not only for the souls but for the minds of his followers. The corollary of a religious revival was an intellectual revival. He set out to make of the Methodists a reading people. Towards the end of his life he thus summarized the conviction of half a century as their leader: 'It cannot be that the people should grow in grace unless they give themselves to reading. A reading people will always be a knowing people.'[4] A major means to this end was *A Collection of Moral and Sacred Poems*, published in three volumes, 1743–44; this began with two extracts from *Paradise Lost*, V.153–208 (entitled 'Morning Hymn', and VII.210–492, 499–534, 548–50 (entitled 'Creation'). In 1745, at his second Conference with his preachers, he arranged that at each of his (and their) headquarters in London, Bristol, and Newcastle there should be small libraries containing copies of Milton. At the Conference of 1746 he inaugurated the ruling that all the preachers should read *Paradise Lost*.[5]

Wesley was also concerned about children's education. In 1739 he embarked on elementary education for colliers' children in the Bristol area, and in 1748 built a school at nearby Kingswood for secondary teaching. In his curriculum for the seventh class appeared the instruction: 'Transcribe and repeat select portions of Milton.'[6] His *Journal* shows that he himself put that ruling into operation on 26 September 1750, and the two following days: 'I reached Kingswood in the evening; and the next day selected passages of Milton for the eldest children to transcribe and repeat weekly.' This was continued at an advanced academic level from 1768 onwards, after some young Methodists had been expelled from Cambridge, Milton being studied during the third year of four.[7]

John Wesley's devotion to Milton, and especially to *Paradise Lost*, is revealed by the multitudinous quotations in his letters and his publications. His sources range over the whole Western literary world, in several languages, with a great fondness for verse, and especially for the Latin classics. In English verse his immense family loyalty (if nothing more) led to hundreds of quotations from his brother Charles, and at least fifty from his older brother Samuel, both of them like himself devotees of Milton. From outside his immediate family there are thirty-one from Pope, including nine from the 'Essay on Man'; there are no fewer than fifty from Prior, including eighteen from *Solomon*, which Charles Wesley advised his daughter Sally to commit to heart. The palm is easily taken, however, by Milton; besides quotations from a handful from other poems, including *Paradise Regained*, there are nearly eighty from *Paradise Lost*.

The influence of Milton on the Wesley family, however, is not limited to these clear – if often imperfect – quotations: their own verses owe a great debt to Milton, and are heavily sprinkled with allusive references to *Paradise Lost* above all other poems. This is especially seen in *A Collection of Hymns for the use of the People called Methodists* (1780). The almost fifty allusions noted in the index to the critical edition of that volume are a mere sample of those in the massive Wesley corpus of verse, and even those fifty are by no means exhaustive of the Miltonic similarities in that volume itself. Here is a rich field for exploration by scholars.[8]

The context of some of Wesley's quotations is in itself revealing. He handles the poem like one who had analysed its parts and language very carefully, although no concordance to Milton was then available. One interesting example is in Discourse V on the Sermon on the Mount (1748), 'Against example, singularly good', where Wesley appears to be conflating *Paradise Lost*, XI.809 ('Against example, good') and *Paradise Regained*, III.57 ('His lot who dares be singularly good'). The situation is made more complex, however, because Wesley's older brother Samuel's own reminiscence of Milton may have been his source, for Samuel had written, 'Against example resolutely good'.[9] Even more impressive is Wesley's ingenious conflation of three lines about Satan, as he described the mental deterioration of Emanuel Swedenborg, where first he changes Milton's 'form' to 'mind': 'His *mind* has not yet lost / All its original brightness, but appears' (I.591–92), and then adds, from II.305, 'Majestic, though in ruin'. The verbal clue to the switch was the word 'ruined' in Milton's I.593: 'Less than an archangel ruined'.[10] In his sermon, 'God's Approbation of His Works' (1782), Wesley quoted Milton nine times, with this tribute in the preamble: 'I do not remember to have seen any attempt of this kind unless in that truly

excellent poem (termed by Mr Hutchinson, "that wretched farce")
Milton's *Paradise Lost.*[11] Wesley undoubtedly regarded Milton as an
expert in eschatology, but he did not swallow him hook, line, and
sinker, as evidenced by his sermon 'On Hell': 'Even the poet who
affirms (though I know not on what authority), "Devil with devil
damned / Firm concord holds", does not affirm that there is any
concord among the human fiends that inhabit the great abyss.' And
later: 'Our great poet himself supposes the inhabitants of hell to
undergo variety of tortures . . . But I find no word, no tittle of this,
not the least hint of it, in all the Bible. And surely this is too awful a
subject to admit of such play of imagination.'[12]

One of the most appropriate and moving of Wesley's quotations
from Milton, however, occurs in his *Journal* for 1 January 1789, a
New Year's reflection a little over two years from his death: 'If this
is to be the last year of my life, according to some of those prophecies,
I hope it will be the best. I am not careful about it, but heartily receive
the advice of the angel in Milton:

How well is thine; how long permit to heaven.'[13]

Throughout most of his mature years John Wesley furnished
reading lists and advice for the more literate Methodists. In his extract
from John Norris, *Reflections upon the Conduct of Human Life, with
Reference to Learning and Knowledge*, first published in 1734, he had
appended 'A Scheme of Books, suited to the Preceding Reflections'
– which did not include Milton. The list was dropped from the 1741
edition, but a new list appeared in 1755, including Milton's *Paradise
Lost*. He recommended 'Milton' to Philothea Briggs in 1771, to Ann
Tindall in 1774, and to his niece Sally Wesley in 1781.[14] In his
Arminian Magazine for November 1780 he offered the Methodist
public in general a reading list which he had prepared for 'Miss L.' –
including, of course, *Paradise Lost*. When in 1787 a preacher's widow
in Ireland lost her own books in a fire Wesley arranged to furnish her
with what he considered at least the nucleus of a good library: 'I
desire Brother Rogers to send her by the first opportunity the Large
Hymn-book, *Notes on the New Testament*, quarto, the *Appeals*, bound,
the four volumes of *Sermons*, Life of Mr Fletcher, of D[avid] Brainerd,
and of Madame Guyon, [Young's] *Night Thoughts*, Milton.'[15]

By 1763 John Wesley and his brother had already published over two
hundred items, and it was natural that John should ponder some

more editorial work upon his favourite poet. It appeared in 1763: *An Extract from Milton's Paradise Lost. With Notes. London: Printed by Henry Fenwick, MDCCLXIII.* To prepare an edited and annotated copy of such a work was certainly a major undertaking, perhaps a perilous one from the point of view of his critics, not all of whom would read his preface (dated 1 January 1763) with sufficient care:

To the Reader

Of all the poems which have hitherto appeared in the world, in whatever age or nation, the preference has generally been given by impartial judges to Milton's *Paradise Lost.* But this inimitable work, amidst all its beauties, is unintelligible to abundance of readers, the immense learning which he has everywhere crowded together making it quite obscure to persons of a common education.

This difficulty, almost insuperable as it appears, I have endeavoured to remove in the following extract: first, by omitting those lines which I despaired of explaining to the unlearned without using abundance of words; and, secondly, by adding short and easy notes, such as I trust will make the main of this excellent poem clear and intelligible to any uneducated person of a tolerable good understanding.

Even a sympathetic Milton scholar such as Walter Herbert exclaimed: 'Milton must have stirred uneasily in his grave. Imagine the shade of the man who sought "fit audience though few" – author of the poem which . . . calls upon all the wealth of bookish information the most scholarly reader can bring to it – looking over Wesley's shoulder as he wrote his preface.' It was certainly not written for the merely intelligent though uneducated persons of the eighteenth century, Wesley's proclaimed audience. Yet Dr Herbert acknowledged that by means of his careful omissions he succeeded remarkably: 'For the unlearned people whom the editor expected to reach the edition was epochal. It brought them one of the greatest of all poems in a form which, though cleared of the thorns which would inevitably have discouraged them, showed them no scars where the pruning knife had cut. No part of the action was lost, and extremely few of the great memorable passages.'[16]

A decade later another Princeton scholar, Oscar Sherwin, was moved to a much fuller study of Wesley's *Paradise Lost,* claiming at the outset: 'Justice has not sufficiently been done to Wesley both for the quantity and variety of his publications or for his pioneer educational work among the masses.'[17] Dr Sherwin showed in detail how Wesley carefully pruned Milton's poem from 10565 lines to 8695, though he also noted that Wesley occasionally erred in his own numbering of the twelve books, so that he appeared to preserve 8708 lines.[18] He categorized the various types of omission by means of passages quoted at length in order 'to reveal the excellence of his method and the splendid readability of his edition'. He omitted strange names, similes, allusions from the classics and even the Bible.[19] He omitted whatever was tortuous and involved, 'geographical or astronomical or historical obscurities', 'omissions to heighten dramatic intensity [or] to simplify text'.[20] Wesley also abridged in order 'to make sentences shorter, clearer, more compact',[21] or to excise passages which he thought immodest or theologically incorrect.[22] Dr Sherwin also pointed out that alterations and additions were 'insignificant in quantity and quality', and the notes 'short and pointed'. His final tribute to Wesley's Milton was that 'in portable and understandable form it made a great classic available to the masses'.

It is indeed true that Wesley's editorial revisions of his abridged Milton were minimal, but they were an important part of his task, which according to Dr Sherwin amounted to sixty-two passages in all. Contrary to a too widespread impression, they involved no halting of the rhythm. Wesley was completely at home with decasyllabic blank verse. Most of his revisions were simple word changes, and an occasional altered phrase. In Milton's lines, 'Satan, who that day / Prodigious power had shown, and met in arms / No equal, ranging through the dire attack / Of fighting Seraphim confused', Wesley combined omission and alteration to read, 'Satan, who that day / Prodigious power had shown, amid the ranks / Of fighting Seraphim confused' (VI.246–49, Wesley's VI.236–38). In VIII.222–23 he smoothed out the grammar and the tenses of 'Speaking, or mute, all comeliness and grace / Attends thee, and each word, each motion, forms', so that it became, 'Speaking or mute all comeliness and grace / Attend thee, and each word, each motion form.'

It is also true that Wesley's annotations in general were laconic. They are fully in line with his *The Complete English Dictionary, explaining most of the Hard Words which are found in the best English*

Writers (1753), of which one entry read: 'A METHODIST, one that lives according to the method laid down in the Bible.' So here we have: '*Monarchy* is Government by One' (I.42); '*Ken* – see, discern' (I.59); '*Pregnant* – Big with future effects' (II.779); '*Panoply* – compleat armour' (VI.527); '*Loquacious*–talkative'(X.161). Many of the notes, especially on classical mythology, are much fuller, and occasionally Wesley's own prejudice creeps in: '*Can make a Heaven of Hell* – This is a fit Rant for a Stoic or a Devil' (I.255). For economy the notes are added in groups at the end of each book, in the same size type as the 322–page pocket volume itself, 7 point, with 2 point leading, too small for comfortable reading, but nothing like as tiny as that of Wesley's Field Bible, from which he preached in the open air.

Having published the work in 1763, Wesley strove to encourage its dissemination. He wrote from Edinburgh to his book steward for the Newcastle area, Matthew Lowes: 'O Matthew, how is this! There is not one *Milton* here, nor one set of the *Philosophy*. Pray send immediately twelve sets of the *Philosophy* and twenty *Miltons* (if you have more than twenty at Newcastle, for you must not be left without some) . . .'. (Lowes added over '*Miltons*' the figure '8', either the number he had at Newcastle or more probably the surplus which he sent to Edinburgh.)[23] The first noted appearance of the volume in his book catalogues was in 1768, among the hymns, as 'Paradise Lost with Notes – 2s.6d.', to which 'b[oun]d' was added in 1770. Clearly it sold only slowly, and by 1777 the price had been reduced to 1s.6d. Thus it continued until Wesley's death. Immediately after the subsequent inventory of the Book Room had turned up no copies it was reprinted, with some revisions of its 335 pages, including the renumbering of the lines. It was advertised as 'Paradise Lost, a new Edition. 2s.'

We have delayed until this point the mention of a unique feature of Wesley's Milton, which later he used for his edition of Young's *Night Thoughts* (1770) and his own collected *Works* (1771–74). A description of this innovation he appended to his preface: 'To those passages which I apprehend to be peculiarly excellent, either with regard to sentiment or expression, I have prefixed a star. And these, I believe, it would be worth while to read over and over, or even to commit to memory.'[24] That Wesley recognized this as a highly unusual practice is made clear by a letter of 10 March 1774 to Thomas Stedman, describing his *Works:* 'It may be needful to mention one thing more, because it is a little out of the common way. In the Extract from Milton's *Paradise Lost* and in that from Dr Young's *Night Thoughts* I placed a mark before those passages which I judged were most worthy of the reader's notice. The same thing I have taken the liberty to do throughout the ensuing volumes.' The device may well have been original, possibly unique – certainly it would be good to know if there were in fact any precedent.

By this usage, of course, Wesley supplied a remarkable guide to his own taste, and furnished what he clearly regarded as the heart of *Paradise Lost*, about a quarter of the original poem. Presumably most of these one hundred and forty-three passages he would himself have memorized, and they should therefore have formed the primary source for his quotations. Examining the tally of quotations recognized so far, this turns out indeed to be the case. Of the seventy-six known quotations forty-nine are from these asterisked passages, i.e. two-thirds of the total. Clearly, however, Wesley himself knew and remembered *Paradise Lost* in far greater detail than he would expect his followers or any non-Methodist readers to memorize; indeed seven of his quoted passages are not even included in his *Extract*. And after all that abridgment surrendered only about one-sixth of the whole poem. The length of Wesley's emphasized passages ranges from one line ('Lives there who loves his pain?' IV.888) to eighty-two (IV.32–113). Wesley usually placed his asterisks at the beginning and the end of selected passages, and his assumption seemed to have been that lengthy passages were to be marked only at the beginning of each paragraph until the last.

This reprinting of the emphasized extracts which comprised for Wesley the heart of *Paradise Lost* has been controlled along lines similar to those of the Bicentennial Edition of *The Works of John Wesley:* obvious errors have been corrected, but no words have been added, omitted, or altered without indication. Occasional editorial insertions of mine are enclosed within square brackets; these are intended to preserve continuity between the passages marked by Wesley, and sometimes to preserve passages where his intentions remain somewhat uncertain. The lines are numbered (usually in fives) on the basis of Milton's numbering, not Wesley's; breaks and ellipses are shown by ' . . .' together with the beginning and ending numbers in the right margin. Like Wesley, I have grouped his annotations at the end of each of Milton's books. Instead of using

'Ver.22', etc., as he did, however, with no clue in the text to the appended notes, I have assigned numbers to those notes which refer to the abridged text, and have added corresponding superscript figures in the text itself.

Frank Baker

Notes to the Introduction

1. Luke Tyerman, *Life and Times of the Rev. John Wesley, M.A.*, 3 vols., Hodder and Stoughton 1870, Vol. I, p. 20. Cf. what appears to be a personal recollection by Adam Clarke of a pronouncement by Wesley, which may well imply the reading aloud of *Paradise Lost* in Epworth rectory: 'My sister Harper [Emilia] was the best reader of Milton I ever heard' (Adam Clarke, *Memoirs of the Wesley Family*, London, Kershaw 1823, p. 469).

2. Cf. Richard P. Heitzenrater, 'John Wesley and the Oxford Methodists, 1725–35', Ph.D. Dissertation, Duke University 1972, pp. 108, 429–30. The first item noted in Wesley's list of his own MSS was Milton.

3. This section was added in one only of several MS Journals – (B).

4. From a letter to a preacher, 8 December 1790. Cf. a letter of 11 February 1773, to John Bredin: 'A reading people will always be a knowing people.'

5. Wesley Historical Society, Publication 1, 'John Bennet's Copy of the Minutes of the Conferences . . .', London 1896, pp. 28–29, 36.

6. *A Short Account of the School in Kingswood*, Bristol 1749, p. 4 (see a facsimile in A. G. Ives, *Kingswood School in Wesley's Day and Since*, Epworth Press 1970, pp. [11–18]).

7. Ives, op. cit., pp. 75, 245–49.

8. See especially Richard Butterworth, 'Milton and the Methodist Hymn Book', *Proceedings* of the Wesley Historical Society, Vol. 10, pp. 97–102 (1915); Samuel J. Rogal, 'The Role of *Paradise Lost* in Works by John and Charles Wesley', *Milton Quarterly*, Vol. 13, pp. 114–19 (1979); James Dale (Department of English, McMaster University, Hamilton, Ontario), 'Milton, Charles Wesley, and the Gospel of Love'; and Elizabeth [Hannon] Hart (University of British Columbia; M.A. thesis, 1985), 'The Influence of *Paradise Lost* on the Hymns of Charles Wesley', which contains a section persuasively pointing out the strong Miltonic influence on the original poem, *The Whole Armour of God* ('Soldiers of Christ, arise').

9. See Wesley's *Sermons*, ed. A. C. Outler, Bicentennial Edition, Abingdon, Nashville, 1984, Vol. 1, p. 569.

10. *Journal*, 8 December 1771. On 22 April 1779, Wesley reverted to Swedenborg's fever and madness at fifty-five, and used the same quotation in the plural, 'majestic, though in ruins'.

11. *Sermons*, Bicentennial Edition, Vol. 2, p. 388.

12. *Sermons*, Bicentennial Edition, Vol. 3, pp. 34–35, 39.

13. Cf. Milton, XI.553–34:

> Nor love thy life, nor hate; but what thou liv'st
> Live well; how long or short permit to heaven.

14. In letters written 25 January 1771, 6 July 1774, and 8 September 1781.

15. Letter to Arthur Keen, 20 April 1787.

16. Thomas Walter Herbert, *John Wesley as Editor and Author*, Princeton University Press 1940, pp. 75–79.

17. Oscar Sherwin, 'Milton for the Masses: John Wesley's Edition of *Paradise Lost*', *Modern Language Quarterly*, Vol. 12, pp. 267–85 (1951).

18. Op. cit., p. 269.

19. Ibid., pp. 270–72.

20. Ibid., pp. 272–79.

21. Ibid., pp. 279–80.

22. Ibid., pp. 280–83.

23. It should be noted that Wesley's two-volume *A Survey of the Wisdom of God in the Creation: or a Compendium of Natural Philosophy* was also published in 1763, and bore a quotation from Milton on its title-page: 'These are thy glorious works, Parent of good . . .' (*Paradise Lost*, V.153–55, Wesley's most frequently-quoted passage).

24. See Frank Baker, 'John Wesley, Literary Arbiter: An Introduction to his use of the Asterisk', *Proceedings* of the Wesley Historical Society Vol.40, pp. 25–33 (1975).

JOHN MILTON

Paradise Lost

Emphasized extracts selected, edited,
and annotated by John Wesley

BOOK I

The Argument

This first book proposes first in brief the whole subject, man's disobedience, and the loss thereupon of Paradise wherein he was placed; then touches the prime cause of his fall, the serpent, or rather Satan in the serpent; who, revolting from God, and drawing to his side many legions of angels, was, by the command of God, driven out of heaven, with all his crew, into the great deep. Which action passed over, the poem hastes into the midst of things, presenting Satan, with his angels, now fallen into hell, described here, not in the centre (for heaven and earth may be supposed as yet not made, certainly not yet accursed), but in a place of utter darkness, fitliest called chaos. Here Satan, with his angels, lying on the burning lake, thunderstruck and astonished, after a certain space recovers, as from confusion, calls up him who, next in order and dignity, lay by him; they confer of their miserable fall. Satan awakens all his legions, who lay till then in the same manner confounded; they rise; their numbers, array of battle, their chief leaders named, according to the idols known afterwards in Canaan and the countries adjoining. To these Satan directs his speech, comforts them with hope yet of regaining heaven, but tells them, lastly, of a new world, and new kind of creature to be created, according to an ancient prophecy or report in heaven; for that angels were long before this visible creation, was the opinion of many ancient fathers. To find out the truth of this prophecy, and what to determine thereon, he refers to a full council. What his associates thence attempt. Pandemonium, the palace of Satan, rises, suddenly built out of the deep: the infernal peers there sit in council.

[Of man's first disobedience, and the fruit
Of that forbidden tree, whose mortal taste

Brought death into the world, and all our woe,
With loss of Eden, till one greater man
Restore us, and regain the blissful seat,   I.5
Sing, heav'nly muse,] . . . O Spir'it, that dost prefer   I.6,17
Before all temples th'upright heart and pure
Instruct me, for thou know'st; thou from the first
Wast present, and with mighty wings outspread   I.20
Dove-like sat'st brooding[1] on the vast abyss,
And mad'st it pregnant; what in me is dark
Illumine,[2] what is low raise and support;
That to the height of this great argument
I may assert eternal providence,   I.25
And justify the ways of God to men.
    Say first – for heav'n hides nothing from thy view,
Nor the deep tract of hell – say first what cause
Moved our grand parents, in that happy state,
Favoured of heav'n so highly, to fall off   I.30
From their Creator, and transgress his will,
For one restraint, lords of the world besides?
Who first seduced them to that foul revolt?
    Th'infernal serpent; he it was, whose guile,
Stirred up with envy and revenge, deceived   I.35
The mother of mankind, what time his pride
Had cast him out from heav'n, with all his host
Of rebel angels, by whose aid aspiring
To set himself in glory 'bove his peers,[3]
He trusted to have equalled the Most High,   I.40
If he opposed; and with ambitious aim
Against the throne and monarchy[4] of God
Raised impious war in heav'n and battle proud
With vain attempt. Him the Almighty Power
Hurled headlong flaming from th'ethereal sky,   I.45
With hideous ruin[5] and combustion, down
To bottomless perdition, there to dwell
In adamantine[6] chains and penal fire,
Who durst defy th'Omnipotent to arms.
    Nine times the space that measures day and night   I.50
To mortal men, he with his horrid crew
Lay vanquished, rolling in the fiery gulf
Confounded though immortal; but his doom

Reserved him to more wrath; for now the thought
Both of lost happiness and lasting pain   I.55
Torments him; round he throws his baleful[7] eyes,
That witnessed huge affliction and dismay
Mixed with obdurate pride and steadfast hate.
At once, as far as angels ken,[8] he views
The dismal situation waste and wild;   I.60
A dungeon horrible on all sides round
As one great furnace flamed, yet from those flames
No light, but rather darkness visible[9]
Served only to discover sights of woe,
Regions of sorrow, doleful shades, where peace   I.65
And rest can never dwell, hope never comes
That comes to all; but torture without end
Still urges, and a fiery deluge, fed
With ever-burning sulphur unconsumed:
Such place eternal justice had prepared   I.70
For those rebellious, here their pris'on ordained
In utter darkness, and their portion set
As far removed from God and light of heaven,
As from the centre[10] thrice to th'utmost pole.
O how unlike the place from whence they fell.   I.75
[There the companions of his fall, o'erwhelmed
With floods and whirlwinds of tempestuous fire,
He soon discerns, and welt'ring by his side
One next himself in pow'r, and next in crime, . . .   I.79
Beelzebub. To whom the arch-enemy   I.81
And thence in heav'n called Satan, with bold words
Breaking the horrid silence thus began:]
   If thou art he; but O how fall'n! how changed
From him who in the happy realms of light,
Clothed with transcendent brightness didst outshine
Myriads[11] though bright! If he whom mutual league,
United thoughts and counsels, equal hope
And hazard in the glorious enterprise,
Joined with me once, now misery hath joined   I.90
In equal ruin; into what pit thou seest
From what height fall'n; so much the stronger proved
He with his thunder; and till then who knew
The force of these dire arms? Yet not for those,

Nor what the potent victor in his rage   I.95
Can else inflict, do I repent or change,
Though changed in outward lustre, that fixed mind,
And high disdain, from sense of injured merit,
That with the mightiest raised me to contend,
And to the fierce contention brought along   I.100
Innumerable force of spirits armed,
That durst dislike his reign, and me preferring,
His utmost pow'r with adverse pow'r opposed
In dubious battle on the plains of heaven,
And shook his throne . . .   I.105
    But what if he our conqu'ror (whom I now
Of force believe almighty, since no less
Than such could have o'erpow'red such force as ours)   I.145
Have left us this our spi'rit and strength entire
Strongly to suffer and support our pains,
That we may so suffice his vengeful ire,
Or do him mightier service as his thralls
By right of war, whate'er his business be,   I.150
Here in the heart of hell to work in fire,
Or do his errands in the gloomy deep?
What can it then avail, though yet we feel
Strength undiminished, or eternal being
To undergo eternal punishment?   I.155
    [Whereto with speedy words the arch-fiend replied:] . . .   I.156
But see, the angry victor hath recalled
His ministers of vengeance[12] and pursuit   I.170
Back to the gates of heav'n; the sulphurous hail
Shot after us in storm, o'erblown hath laid
The fiery surge, that from the precipice
Of heav'n received us falling; and the thunder,
Winged with red lightning and impetuous rage,   I.175
Perhaps hath spent his shafts, and ceases now
To bellow through the vast and boundless deep.
Let us not slip the occasion, whether scorn
Or satiate fury yield it from our foe.
Seest thou yon dreary[13] plain, forlorn and wild,   I.180
The seat of desolation, void of light,
Save what the glimmering of these livid[14] flames
Casts pale and dreadful? Thither let us tend

From off the tossing of these fiery waves;
There rest, if any rest can harbour there . . .   I.185
   Thus Satan talking to his nearest mate   I.192
With head uplift above the wave, and eyes
That sparkling blazed, his other parts besides
Prone on the flood, extended long and large
Lay floating many a rood;[15] . . . nor ever thence   I.196,210
Had ris'n or heaved his head, but that the will
And high permission of all-ruling heaven
Left him at large to his own dark designs . . .
   Forthwith upright he rears from off the pool   I.221
His mighty stature; on each hand the flames
Driv'n backward slope their pointing spires, and rolled
In billows, leave i'th' midst a horrid vale.
Then with expanded[16] wings he steers his flight   I.225
Aloft, incumbent on the dusky air
That felt unusual weight, till on dry land
He lights, if it were land that ever burned
With solid, as the lake with liquid fire . . .   I.229
   Is this the region, this the soil, the clime,   I.242
Said then the lost archangel, this the seat
That we must change for heav'n, this mournful gloom
For that celestial light? Be it so, since he   I.245
Who now is Sov'reign can dispose and bid
What shall be right: farthest from him is best,
Whom reas'on hath equalled, force hath made supreme
Above his equals. Farewell, happy fields,
Where joy for ever dwells; hail, horrors, hail   I.250
Infernal world, and thou profoundest hell
Receive thy new possessor; one who brings
A mind not to be changed by place or time.
The mind is its own place, and in itself
Can make a heav'n of hell,[17] a hell of heav'n . . .   I.255
   He scarce had ceased when the superior fiend   I.283
Was moving tow'ard the shore; his pond'rous shield,
Ethereal[18] temper, massy, large and round   I.285
Behind him cast; the broad circumference
Hung on his shoulders like the moon, whose orb
Through optic glass the Tuscan artist[19] views . . .   I.288
His spear, to equal which the tallest pine   I.292

Hewn on Norwegian hills were but a wand,
He walked with to support uneasy steps
Over the burning marle (not like those steps   I.295
On heaven's azure), and the torrid clime[20]
Smote on him sore besides, vaulted with fire:
Nathless[21] he so endured, till on the beach
Of that inflamed sea he stood, and called   I.300
His legions, angel forms, who lay entranced
Thick as autumnal leaves that strow the brooks
In Vallombrosa,[22] where th'Etrurian shades
High over-arched embow'r; . . . so thick bestrown,   I.304,311
Abject and lost lay these, covering the flood,
Under amazement of their hideous change.
He called so loud that all the hollow deep
Of hell resounded: Princes, Potentates,   I.315
Warriors, the flower of heav'n, once yours, now lost,
If such astonishment as this can seize
Eternal spi'rits; or have ye chos'n this place
After the toil of battle to repose
Your wearied virtue, for the ease you find   I.320
To slumber here, as in the vales of heaven?
Or in this abject posture have ye sworn
To'adore the Conqueror? Who now beholds
Cherub and Seraph rolling in the flood
With scattered arms and ensigns, till anon   I.325
His swift pursuers from heav'n gates discern
Th'advantage, and descending tread us down
Thus, drooping, or with linked thunderbolts
Transfix us to the bottom of this gulf.
Awake, arise, or be for ever fall'n!   I.330
   [They heard, and were abashed, and up they sprung
Upon the wing . . . who . . . had general names   I.332,421
Of Baalim and Ashtaroth, those male,]
These feminine. For spirits when they please   I.423
Can either sex assume, or both; so soft
And uncompounded is their essence pure,
Not tied or manacled with joint or limb
Nor founded on the brittle strength of bones,
Like cumbrous flesh; but in what shape they choose,
Dilated or condensed, bright or obscure,   I.430

Can execute their airy purposes
And works of love or enmity fulfil . . .
                Anon they move . . .   I.549
To flutes and soft recorders; such as raised   I.551
To height of noblest tempers heroes old
Arming to battle, and instead of rage
Deliberate valour breathed, firm and unmoved
With dread of death to flight or foul retreat;   I.555
Nor wanting pow'r to mitigate and swage
With solemn touches troubled thoughts, and chase
Anguish, and doubt, and fear, and sorrow, and pain
From mortal or immortal minds . . . [These far beyond I.559,587
Compare of mortal prowess, yet observed]
Their dread commander: he above the rest . . .   I.589
Stood like a tow'r; his form had yet not lost   I.591
All her original brightness, nor appeared
Less than archangel ruined, and th'excess
Of glory obscured. As when the sun new risen
Looks through the horizontal[23] misty air   I.595
Shorn of his beams, or from behind the moon
In dim eclipse disastrous twilight sheds
On half the nations, and with fear of change
Perplexes monarchs. Darkened so, yet shone
Above them all th'archangel; but his face   I.600
Deep scars of thunder had entrenched, and care
Sat on his faded cheek, but under brows
Of dauntless courage, and considerate pride
Waiting revenge; cruel his eye, but cast
Signs of remorse and passion to behold   I.605
The fellows of his crime, the followers rather
(Far other once beheld in bliss) condemned
For ever now to have their lot in pain,
Millions of spirits for his fault amerced[24]
Of heav'n, and from eternal splendours flung   I.610
For his revolt – yet faithful how they stood,
Their glory withered; as when heaven's fire
Hath scathed[25] the forest oaks, or mountain pines,
With singed top their stately growth, though bare,
Stands on the blasted heath. He now prepared   I.615
To speak; whereat their doubled ranks they bend

From wing to wing, and half enclose him round
With all his peers. Attention held them mute.
Thrice he essayed, and thrice, in spite of scorn,
Tears, such as angels weep, burst forth: at last   I.620
Words interwove with sighs found out their way . . .
    He spake; and to confirm his words, out-flew   I.663
Millions of flaming swords, drawn from the thighs
Of mighty Cherubim; the sudden blaze
Far round illumined hell; highly they raged
Against the high'est, and fierce with grasped arms
Clashed on their sounding shields the din of war,
Hurling defiance to'ward the vault of heaven.   I.669

Notes on Book I

  1. *Dove-like sat'st brooding.* This is the proper meaning of the word, which is translated *moved*, Gen. 1:2.
  2. *Illumine* – enlighten.
  3. *Above his peers* – his fellow angels, even to be equal with God.
  4. *Monarchy* is government by one.
  5. *Ruin* – falling with violence; *combustion* – burning in a dreadful manner.
  6. *Adamantine* – firm like diamond.
  7. *Baleful* – full of woe or mischief.
  8. *Ken* – see, discern.
  9. *Darkness visible* – a dark gloom.
  10. *From the centre* of the Earth to the outermost point of it.
  11. A *myriad* is ten thousand.
  12. *His ministers of vengeance.* To veil his shame, Satan ascribes his fall to the whole host of angels; but Raphael, VI.157, to the Messiah alone.
  13. *Dreary* – dismal.
  14. *Livid* – bluish.
  15. A *rood* is two hundred and twenty yards.
  16. *Expanded* – stretched out.
  17. *Can make a heav'n of hell.* This is a fit rant for a stoic or a devil.
  18. *Ethereal* – heavenly.
  19. *The Tuscan artist* – Galileo, a native of Tuscany.
  20. *The torrid clime* – the scorching climate.
  21. *Nathless* – nevertheless.
  22. *Vallombrosa* – that is, a shady valley, a valley in Tuscany, formerly called Hetruria.
  23. *Horizontal* – near the horizon, the line where the sky and Earth seem to meet.
  24. *Amerced of heav'n* – punished with the loss of it.
  25. *Scathed* – struck, hurt, scorched.

BOOK II

The Argument

The consultation begun, Satan debates whether another battle be to be hazarded for the recovery of heaven: some advise it, others dissuade. A third proposal is preferred, mentioned before by Satan, to search the truth of that prophecy or tradition in heaven concerning another world, and another kind of creature equal or not much inferior to themselves, about this time to be created. Their doubt who shall be sent on this difficult search. Satan their chief undertakes alone the voyage, is honoured and applauded. The council thus ended, the rest betake themselves several ways, and to several employments, as their inclinations lead them, to entertain the time till Satan return. He passes on his journey to hell gates, finds them shut, and who sat there to guard them, by whom at length they are opened, and discover to him the great gulf between hell and heaven. With what difficulty he passes through, directed by Chaos, the power of that place, to the sight of this new world which he sought.

[Moloch, sceptred king, stood up:]	II.43–44
. . . What can be worse	II.85
Than to dwell here, driv'n out from bliss, condemned	
In this abhorred deep to utter woe;	
Where pain of unextinguishable fire	
Must exercise us without hope of end,	
The vassals of his anger, when the scourge	II.90
Inexorably, and the torturing hour,	
Calls us to penance? More destroyed than thus,	
We should be quite abolished and expire.	
What fear we then? What doubt we to incense	
His utmost ire? Which to the height enraged,	II.95
Will either quite consume us, and reduce	

To nothing this essential – happier far
Than miserable to have eternal being . . .
   He ended frowning, and his look denounced   II.106
Desp'rate revenge, and battle dangerous
To less than gods. On th' other side up rose
Belial, in act more graceful and humane.
A fairer person lost not heav'n; he seemed   II.110
For dignity composed and high exploit.
But all was false and hollow; though his tongue
Dropped manna, and could make the worse appear
The better reason, to perplex and dash
Maturest counsels: for his thoughts were low –   II.115
To vice industrious, but to nobler deeds
Timorous and slothful. Yet he pleased the ear,
And with persuasive accent thus began.
   . . . And that must end us, that must be our cure – II.145
To be no more. Sad cure! for who would lose,
Though full of pain, this intellectual being,
These thoughts that wander through eternity,
To perish rather, swallowed up and lost
In the wide womb of uncreated night,   II.150
Devoid of sense and motion? . . .
[What when we fled amain, pursued and struck   II.165
With heav'n's afflicting thunder, and besought
The deep to shelter us? This hell then seemed
A refuge from those wounds. Or when we lay
Chained on the burning lake? That sure was worse.]
   What if the breath that kindled those grim fires   II.170
Awaked should blow them into sev'nfold rage
And plunge us in the flames? Or from above
Should intermitted vengeance arm again
His red right hand to plague us? What if all
Her stores were opened, and this firmament   II.175
Of hell should spout her cataracts of fire,
Impendent horrors, threat'ning hideous fall
One day upon our heads; while we perhaps
Designing or exhorting glorious war,
Caught in a fiery tempest shall be hurled   II.180
Each on his rock transfixed, the sport and prey
Of racking whirlwinds, or for ever sunk

Under yon boiling ocean, wrapt in chains;
There to converse with everlasting groans,
Unrespited, unpitied, unreprieved,   II.185
Ages of hopeless end? This would be worse . . .
   [Thus Belial with words clothed in reason's garb   II.226
Counselled ignoble ease, and peaceful sloth,
Not peace: and after him thus Mammon spake.]
              . . . This deep world   II.262
Of darkness do we dread? How oft amidst
Thick clouds and dark doth heav'n's all-ruling Sire
Choose to reside, his glory unobscured,   II.265
And with the majesty of darkness round
Covers his throne; from whence deep thunders roar
Must'ring their rage, and heav'n resembles hell? . . .
He scarce had finished, when such murmur filled
Th' assembly, as when hollow rocks retain   II.285
The sound of blust'ring winds, which all night long
Had roused the sea, now with hoarse cadence lull
Seafaring men o'erwatched, whose bark by chance
Or pinnace anchors in a craggy bay
After the tempest. Such applause was heard   II.290
As Mammon ended, and his sentence pleased,
Advising peace: for such another field
They dreaded worse than hell, so much the fear
Of thunder and the sword of Michael
Wrought still within them; and no less desire   II.295
To found this nether empire, which might rise
By policy, and long process of time,
In emulation opposite to heaven.
Which when Beelzebub perceived – than whom,
Satan except, none higher sat – with grave   II.300
Aspect he rose, and in his rising seemed
A pillar of state; deep on his front engraven
Deliberation sat and public care;
And princely counsel in his face yet shone,
Majestic though in ruin. Sage he stood   II.305
With Atlantean[1] shoulders fit to bear
The weight of mightiest monarchies; his look
Drew audience and attention still as night
Or summer's noontide air,[2] while thus he spake . . .

[Satan, whom now transcendent glory raised   II.427
Above his fellows, with monarchal pride,
Conscious of highest worth, unmoved thus spake.]
    O progeny[3] of heav'n, empyreal thrones,   II.430
With reason hath deep silence and demur
Seized us, though undismayed. Long is the way
And hard, that out of hell leads up to light;
Our prison strong; this huge convex[4] of fire
Outrageous to devour, immures[5] us round   II.435
Ninefold, and gates of burning adamant
Barred over us prohibit all egress.[6]
These passed, if any pass, the void profound
Of unessential[7] night receives him next
Wide gaping, and with utter loss of being   II.440
Threatens him, plunged in that abortive[8] gulf.
    If thence he 'scape into whatever world,
Or unknown region, what remains him less
Than unknown dangers, and as hard escape?
But I should ill become this throne, O peers,   II.445
And this imperial sov'reignty, adorned
With splendour, armed with power, if aught proposed
And judged of public moment in the shape
Of difficulty or danger could deter
Me from attempting. Wherefore do I assume   II.450
These royalties, and not refuse to reign,
Refusing to accept as great a share
Of hazard as of honour, due alike
To him who reigns, and so much to him due
Of hazard more, as he above the rest   II.455
High honoured sits? . . .
    Their rising all at once was as the sound   II.476
Of thunder heard remote . . .
    As when from mountain tops the dusky clouds
Ascending, while the north wind sleeps, o'erspread
Heav'n's cheerful face, the louring element   II.490
Scowls o'er the darkened landskip snow, or shower;
If chance the radiant sun with farewell sweet
Extend his evening beam, the fields revive,
The birds their notes renew, and bleating herds
Attest their joy, that hill and valley rings.   II.495

O shame to men! devil with devil damned
Firm concord holds, men only disagree
Of creatures rational, though under hope
Of heav'nly grace, and God proclaiming peace,
Yet live in hatred, enmity, and strife   II.500
Among themselves, and levy cruel wars,
Wasting the earth, each other to destroy! . . .
    Others more mild, in silent valley, sing   II.546–547
With notes angelical to many a harp
Their own heroic deeds and hapless fall
By doom of battle; and complain that fate   II.550
Free virtue should enthral to force or chance.
Their song was partial, but the harmony
(What could it less when spirits immortal sing?)
Suspended hell, and took with ravishment
The thronging audience. In discourse more sweet   II.555
(For eloquence the soul, song charms the sense),
Others apart sat on a hill retired,
In thoughts more elevate, and reasoned high
Of providence, foreknowledge, will, and fate,
Fixed fate, free will, foreknowledge absolute,   II.560
And found no end,[9] in wand'ring mazes lost . . .
    Yet with a pleasing sorcery could charm   II.566
Pain for a while or anguish, and excite
Fallacious hope, or arm th' obdured breast
With stubborn patience as with triple steel.   II.569
Another part in squadrons and gross bands,[10]   II.570
On bold adventure to discover wide
That dismal world, if any clime perhaps
Might yield them easier habitation, bend
Four ways their flying march, along the banks
Of four infernal rivers,[11] that disgorge   II.575
Into the burning lake their baleful streams:
Abhorred Styx, the flood of deadly hate;
Sad Acheron of sorrow, black and deep;
Cocytus, named of lamentation loud
Heard on the rueful stream; fierce Phlegeton,   II.580
Whose waves of torrent fire inflame with rage . . .
Beyond this flood a frozen continent   II.586
Lies dark and wild, beat with perpetual storms

Of whirlwind and dire hail, which on firm land
Thaws not, but gathers heap . . .; the parching air   II.590, 594
Burns frore,[12] and cold performs th' effect of fire.   II.595
Thither, by harpy-footed[13] Furies haled,
At certain revolutions all the damned
Are brought; and feel by turns the bitter change
Of fierce extremes, extremes by change more fierce,
From beds of raging fire to starve in ice   II.600
Their soft ethereal warmth, and there to pine
Immovable, infixed, and frozen round,
Periods of time, thence hurried back to fire . . .   II.603
Thus roving on forlorn, th' advent'rous bands   II.614–615
With shudd'ring horror pale, and eyes aghast,
Viewed first their lamentable lot, and found
No rest. Through many a dark and dreary vale
They passed, and many a region dolorous,[14]
O'er many a frozen, many a fiery alp,[15]   II.620
Rocks, caves, lakes, fens, bogs, dens, and shades of death –
An universe of death, which God by curse
Created evil, for evil only good,
Where all life dies, death lives, and nature breeds,
Perverse, all monstrous, all prodigious things,   II.625
Abominable, inutterable, and worse
Than fables yet have feigned or fear conceived . . .   II.627
    Meanwhile the adversary of God and man,
Satan with thoughts inflamed of highest design,   II.630
Puts on swift wings, and towards the gates of hell
Explores[16] his solitary flight; sometimes
He scours the right-hand coast, sometimes the left,
Now shaves with level wing the deep, then soars
Up to the fiery concave tow'ring high . . .   II.635
At last appear . . . hell bounds, high to the roof,   II.643–644
And thrice threefold the gates; three folds were brass,
Three iron, three of adamantine rock,
Impenetrable, impaled[17] with circling fire,
Yet unconsumed. Before the gates there sat
On either side a formidable shape.
The one seemed woman to the waist, and fair,   II.650
But ended foul in many a scaly fold,
Voluminous and vast, a serpent armed

With mortal sting; about her middle round
A cry[18] of hell-hounds never ceasing rung   II.654–655
A hideous peal; yet, when they list, would creep,
If aught disturbed their noise, into her womb,
Yet there still barked and howled . . . The other shape, II.658, 666
If shape it might be called that shape had none
Distinguishable in member, joint, or limb;
Or substance might be called that shadow seemed,
For each seemed either; black it stood as night . . .   II.670
And shook a dreadful dart; what seemed his head   II.672
The likeness of a kingly crown had on.
Satan was now at hand, and from his seat
The monster moving onward came as fast
With horrid strides; hell trembled as he strode . . .   II.676
So spake the grisly terror, and in shape,   II.704
So speaking and so threat'ning, grew tenfold
More dreadful and deform. On th' other side
Incensed with indignation Satan stood
Unterrified . . . [Meantime] each at the head   II.708,711
Levelled his deadly aim; their fatal hands
No second stroke intend; and such a frown
Each cast at th'other as when two black clouds,
With heav'n's artillery fraught, come rattling on . . .   II.715
Hovering a space, till winds the signal blow   II.717
To join their dark encounter in mid air.
So frowned the mighty combatants, that hell
Grew darker at their frown; so matched they stood;   II.720
For never but once more was either like
To meet so great a foe . . .
    [She finished; and the subtle fiend his lore   II.815
Soon learned, now milder, and thus answered smooth:
Dear daughter, since thou claim'st me for thy sire . . .
I come no enemy, but to set free   II.822
From out this dark and dismal house of pain
Both him and thee, and all the heav'nly host
Of spirits, that in our just pretences armed
Fell with us from on high . . .
Thus saying, from her side the fatal key,   II.871
Sad instrument of all our woe, she took . . .
     . . . then in the keyhole turns   II.876

The intricate wards, and every bolt and bar]
Of massy ir'on or solid rock with ease
Unfastens; on a sudden open fly
With impetuous recoil and jarring sound   II.880
Th' infernal doors, and on their hinges grate
Harsh thunder, that the lowest bottom shook
Of Erebus.[19] She opened, but to shut
Excelled her pow'r; the gates wide opened stood,
That with extended wings a bannered host   II.885
Under spread ensigns marching might pass through
With horse and chariots ranked in loose array;
So wide they stood, and like a furnace mouth
Cast forth redounding[20] smoke and ruddy flame.
Before their eyes in sudden view appear   II.890
The secrets of the hoary[21] deep, a dark
Illimitable[22] ocean, without bound,
Without dimension,[23] where length, breadth, and height,
And time, and place, are lost; where eldest Night
And Chaos, ancestors of Nature,[24] hold   II.895
Eternal anarchy, amidst the noise
Of endless wars . . . Into this wild abyss,   II.897,910
The womb of nature and perhaps her grave,
Of neither sea, nor shore, nor air, nor fire,
But all these in their pregnant[25] causes mixed
Confus'dly, and which thus must ever fight,
Unless th'Almighty Maker them ordain   II.915
His dark material to create more worlds;
Into this wild abyss the wary fiend
Stood on the brink of hell and looked awhile,
Pond'ring his voyage; for no narrow frith[26]
He had to cross. Nor was his ear less pealed   II.920
With noises ruinous[27] . . . than if this frame   II.921,924
Of heav'n were falling, and these elements
In mutiny had from her axle[28] torn
The steadfast Earth. At last his sail-broad vans[29]
He spreads for flight, and in the surging[30] smoke
Uplifted spurns the ground; thence many a league,
As in a cloudy chair, ascending rides   II.930
Audacious; but that seat soon failing, meets
A vast vacuity; all unawares,

Fluttering his pennons vain, plumb down he drops
Ten thousand fathoms deep . . .
       . . . When straight behold the throne   II.959
Of Chaos, and his dark pavilion spread
Wide on the wasteful deep; with him enthroned
Sat sable-vested Night, eldest of things,
The consort of his reign; and by them . . . Chance   II.963,965
And Tumult and Confusion all embroiled,
And Discord with a thousand various mouths . . .
     But now at last the sacred influence   II.1034
Of light appears, and from the walls of heaven
Shoots far into the bosom of dim Night
A glimmering dawn; here Nature first begins
Her farthest verge, and Chaos to retire
As from her utmost works a broken foe,
With tumult less and with less hostile din,   II.1040
That Satan with less toil, and now with ease,
Wafts on the calmer wave by dubious light . . .
Or in the emptier waste, resembling air,   II.1045
Weighs his spread wings, at leisure to behold
Far off th' empyreal heav'n, extended wide . . .
With opal tow'rs[31] and battlements adorned   II.1049
Of living sapphire, once his native seat;
And fast by, hanging in a golden chain,
This pendent world,[32] in bigness as a star
Of smallest magnitude close by the moon . . .   II.1053

Notes on Book II

1. Mount *Atlas* is always covered with clouds. Hence the fable of Atlas bearing the skies on his shoulders.
2. In many countries it is generally calm about *noon*, especially in *summer*.
3. *Progeny* – offspring.
4. *Convex* – the vault bending round us.
5. *Immures us* – walls us in.
6. *Egress* – going out.
7. *Unessential* – uncreated, void of being.
8. *Abortive.* An *abortion* is properly a miscarriage. The word therefore is strongly figurative. Nor is it easy to give it a determinate meaning.
9. *And found no end.* There is no end of *reasoning* concerning these things. Happy therefore are they who simply keep to the Bible.

10. [II.569 ends with an asterisk, as does II.627. It is uncertain where Wesley intended to place the intervening initial asterisk, but II.570 is quite possible.]

11. *Styx, Acheron*, etc. These were, according to the heathen poets, the four rivers of hell.

12. *Burns frore. Frore* is an old word for frosty.

13. *Harpy-footed* – with sharp claws, like the fabled *harpies*, whom the heathen poets described as having eagles' talons. *Furies* – devils assuming the most dreadful shapes.

14. *Dolorous* – sad.

15. *Alp* – mountain, high as the *Alps*.

16. *Explores* – tries, searches out.

17. *Impaled* – surrounded.

18. [Wesley, 'crew'.]

19. *Erebus* – hell.

20. *Redounding* – spreading every way in curling waves.

21. *Hoary* – that is, old. *Secrets* – never seen before by any creature.

22. *Illimitable* – unbounded.

23. *Without dimension.* So empty space must needs be.

24. *Ancestors of Nature.* The ancient poets describe Night or Darkness, and Chaos or Confusion, as the first of things, and exercising uncontrolled dominion from the beginning. In how masterly a manner does Milton paint this! *Anarchy* is just the reverse of regular government.

25. *Pregnant* – big with future effects.

26. A *frith* is an arm of the sea.

27. *Noises ruinous* – of things rushing to and fro.

28. *Her axle.* The Earth moves round every 24 hours, as a wheel on its axle-tree.

29. *Vans* – wings.

30. *Surging* – rising.

31. *Opal towers* – towers of precious stones. An opal is a precious stone of various colours.

32. *This pendent world* – not the Earth, but the whole Universe. And even this, at so vast a distance, appeared as one of the smallest Stars. He does not see the Earth till some time after.

BOOK III

The Argument

God sitting on his throne sees Satan flying towards this world, then newly created; shows him to the Son, who sat at his right hand; foretells the success of Satan in perverting mankind; clears his own justice and wisdom from all imputation, having created man free, and able enough to have withstood his tempter; yet declares his purpose of grace towards him, in regard he fell not of his own malice, as did Satan, but by him seduced. The Son of God renders praises to his Father for the manifestation of his gracious purpose towards man; but God again declares that grace cannot be extended towards man without the satisfaction of divine justice; man hath offended the majesty of God by aspiring to Godhead, and therefore, with all his progeny, devoted to death must die, unless someone can be found sufficient to answer for his offence, and undergo his punishment. The Son of God freely offers himself a ransom for man; the Father accepts him, ordains his incarnation, pronounces his exaltation above all names in heaven and earth; commands all the angels to adore him; they obey, and hymning to their harps in full choir, celebrate the Father and the Son. Meanwhile Satan alights upon the bare convex of this world's outermost orb; where wandering he first finds a place since called the limbo of vanity; what persons and things fly up thither; thence comes to the gate of heaven, described ascending by stairs, and the waters above the firmament that flow about it: his passage thence to the orb of the sun; he finds there Uriel the regent of that orb, but first changes himself into the shape of a meaner angel; and pretending a zealous desire to behold the new creation, and man whom God had placed here, inquires of him the place of his habitation, and is directed; alights first on Mount Niphates.

Hail, holy Light, offspring of heav'n first-born,   III.1
Or of th'Eternal coeternal beam!
May I express thee unblamed? Since God is light,
And never but in unapproached light
Dwelt from eternity, dwelt then in thee   III.5
Bright effluence of bright essence increate.
Or hear'st thou rather pure ethereal stream,
Whose fountain who shall tell? Before the sun,
Before the heav'ns thou wert, and at the voice
Of God, as with a mantle didst invest   III.10
The rising world of waters dark and deep,
Won from the void and formless infinite.
Thee I revisit now with bolder wing . . .   III.13
And feel thy sovereign vital lamp; but thou   III.22
Revisit'st not these eyes, that roll in vain
To find thy piercing ray, and find no dawn;
So thick a drop serene[1] hath quenched their orbs,
Or dim suffusion veiled. Yet not the more
Cease I to wander, where the muses haunt
Clear spring, or shady grove, or sunny hill,
Smit with the love of sacred song; but chief
Thee, Sion, and the flow'ry brooks beneath   III.30
That wash thy hallowed feet, and warbling flow,
Nightly I visit; . . . as the wakeful bird   III.32,38
Sings darkling, and in shadiest covert hid
Tunes her nocturnal note. Thus with the year
Seasons return, but not to me returns
Day, or the sweet approach of ev'n or morn,
Or sight of vernal bloom, or summer's rose,
Or flocks, or herds, or human face divine;
But clouds instead, and ever-during dark   III.45
Surrounds me, from the cheerful ways of men
Cut off, and for the book of knowledge fair
Presented with a universal blank
Of nature's work to me expunged and rased,
And wisdom at one entrance quite shut out.   III.50
So much the rather thou, celestial light,
Shine inward, and the mind through all her powers
Irradiate,[2] there plant eyes, all mist from thence
Purge and disperse, that I may see and tell

Of things invisible to mortal sight . . .   III.55
  [*On Satan*]   [. . . so will fall
He and his faithless progeny: Whose fault?]
Whose but his own? Ingrate, he had of me   III.97
All he could have: I made him just and right,
Sufficient to have stood, though free to fall.
Such I created all th'ethereal powers   III.100
And spirits, both them who stood and them who failed;
Freely they stood who stood, and fell who fell.
Not free, what proof could they have giv'n sincere
Of true allegiance, constant faith or love,
Where only what they needs must do appeared,   III.105
Not what they would? What praise could they receive?
What pleasure I from such obedience paid,
When will and reason (reason also is choice)
Useless and vain, of freedom both despoiled,
Made passive both, had served necessity,   III.110
Not me? They therefore as to right belonged,
So were created, nor can justly' accuse
Their Maker, or their making, or their fate,
As if predestination over-ruled
Their will, disposed by absolute decree   III.115
Of high foreknowledge; they themselves decreed
Their own revolt, not I; if I foreknew,
Foreknowledge had no influence on their fault,
Which had no less proved certain unforeknown.
So without least impulse of shadow' of fate,   III.120
Or aught by me immutably foreseen,
They trespass, authors to themselves in all,
Both what they judge and what they choose; for so
I formed them free, and free they must remain,
Till they enthral themselves; I else must change   III.125
Their nature, and revoke the high decree
Unchangeable, eternal, which ordained
Their freedom, they themselves ordained their fall.
The first sort by their own suggestion fell,
Self-tempted, self-depraved: man falls, deceived   III.130
By th'other first: man therefore shall find grace,
That other none: in mercy' and justice both,
Through heav'n and earth, so shall my glory excel,

But mercy first and last shall brightest shine . . .   III.134
[Man shall not quite be lost, but saved who will,]
Yet not of will in him, but grace in me   III.174
Freely vouchsafed; once more I will renew
His lapsed pow'rs, forfeit and enthalled
By sin to foul exorbitant desires;
Upheld by me, yet once more he shall stand
On even ground against his mortal foe,
By me upheld, that he may know how frail   III.180
His fall'n condition is, and to me owe
All his deliverance, and to none but me . . .   III.182
[For all] shall hear me call, and oft be warned   III.185
Their sinful state, and to appease betimes
Th'incensed deity, while offered grace
Invites; for I will soften stony hearts   III.188–89
To pray, repent, and bring obedience due.
To pray'r, repentance, and obedience due,
Though but endeavoured with sincere intent,
Mine ear shall not be slow, mine eye not shut.
And I will place within them as a guide
My umpire[3] conscience, whom if they will hear,   III.195
Light after light well used they shall attain,
And to the end persisting, safe arrive.
This my long sufferance and my day of grace
They who neglect and scorn shall never taste;
But hard be hardened, blind be blinded more,
And none but such from mercy I exclude . . .   III.202
    Father, thy word is passed, man shall find grace;   III.227
And shall grace not find means, that finds her way
The speediest of thy winged messengers,
To visit all thy creatures, and to all   III.230
Comes unprevented, unimplored, unsought?
Happy for man, so coming; he her aid
Can never seek, once dead in sins and lost –
Atonement for himself, or offering meet,
Indebted and undone, hath none to bring.   III.235
Behold *me*, then; me for him, life for life
I offer; on me let thine anger fall;
Account me man; I for his sake will leave
Thy bosom, and this glory next to thee

Freely put off, and for him lastly die   III.240
Well pleased; on me let death wreak all his rage.
Under his gloomy pow'r I shall not long
Lie vanquished. Thou hast giv'n me to possess
Life in myself for ever; By thee I live,
Though now to death I yield, and am his due,   III.245
All that of me can die; yet that debt paid,
Thou wilt not leave me in the loathsome grave
His prey, nor suffer my unspotted soul
For ever with corruption there to dwell;
But I shall rise victorious, and subdue   III.250
My vanquisher, spoiled of his vaunted spoil . . .
   [Th'Almighty thus replied:] . . .   III.273
Thou therefore, whom thou only canst redeem,   III.281
Their nature also to thy nature join;
And be thyself man among men on earth,
Made flesh, when time shall be, of virgin seed,
By wondrous birth; be thou in Adam's room   III.285
The head of all mankind, though Adam's son.
As in him perish all men, so in thee,
As from a second root, shall be restored
As many as are restored, without thee none.
His crime makes guilty all his sons; thy merit   III.290
Imputed shall absolve them who renounce
Their own both righteous and unrighteous deeds,
And live in thee transplanted, and from thee
Receive new life. So man, as is most just,
Shall satisfy for man, be judged and die,
And dying rise, and rising with him raise
His brethren, ransomed with his own dear life . . .   III.297
   [No sooner had th'Almighty ceased but all   III.344
The multitude of angels gave a shout
Loud as from numbers without number, sweet
As from blest voices, uttering joy, heav'n rung
With jubilee, and loud hosannas filled
Th'eternal regions . . .]   III.349
   Thee, Father, first they sung, Omnipotent   III.372
Immutable, Immortal, Infinite,
Eternal King; thee, Author of all being,
Fountain of light, thyself invisible

(Amidst the glorious brightness where thou sitt'st
Throned inaccessible) but when thou shad'st
The full blaze of thy beams; then through a cloud
Drawn round about thee like a radiant shrine,
Dark with excessive bright thy skirts appear,   III.380
Yet dazzle heav'n, that brightest seraphim
Approach not, but with both wings veil their eyes.
Thee next they sang of all creation first,
Begotten Son, divine Similitude,
In whose conspicuous count'nance, without cloud   III.385
Made visible, th'Almighty Father shines,
Whom else no creature can behold; on thee
Impressed th'effulgence of his glory' abides,
Transfused on thee his ample Spirit rests.
He heav'n of heav'ns, and all the pow'rs therein,   III.390
By thee created, and by thee threw down
Th'aspiring Dominations. Thou that day
Thy Father's dreadful thunder didst not spare,
Nor stop thy flaming chariot wheels, that shook
Heav'n's everlasting frame, while o'er the necks   III.395
Thou drov'st of warring angels disarrayed.
Back from pursuit, thy pow'rs with loud acclaim
Thee only extolled,[4] Son of thy Father's might,
To execute fierce vengeance on his foes.
Not so on man: him, through their malice fallen,   III.400
Father of mercy' and grace, thou didst not doom
So strictly, but much more to pity inclined.
No sooner did thy dear and only Son
Perceive thee purposed not to doom frail man
So strictly, but much more to pity' incline,   III.405
He, to appease thy wrath, and end the strife
Of mercy and justice in thy face discerned,
Regardless of the bliss wherein he sat
Second to thee, offered himself to die
For man's offence. O unexampled love,   III.410
Love nowhere to be found less than divine!
Hail, Son of God, Saviour of men! Thy name
Shall be the copious matter of my song
Henceforth, and never shall my harp thy praise
Forget, nor from they Father's praise disjoin . . .   III.415

[Meanwhile upon the firm opacous globe . . .   III.418
Satan alighted walks . . .   III.422
Saw within ken a glorious angel stand,   III.622
The same whom John saw also in the sun.]
His back was turned, but not his brightness hid!
Of beaming sunny rays a golden tiar[5]
Circled his head, nor less his locks behind
Illustrious on his shoulders fledge with wings
Lay waving round; on some great charge employed
He seemed, or fixed in cogitation[6] deep . . .   III.629
So spake the false dissembler unperceived;   III.681
For neither man nor angel can discern
Hypocrisy – the only evil that walks
Invisible except to God alone,
By his permissive will, through heav'n and earth;   III.685
And oft, though wisdom wake, suspicion sleeps
At wisdom's gate, and to simplicity
Resigns her charge, while goodness thinks no ill
Where no ill seems: [which now for once beguiled   III.689
Uriel, though regent of the sun, and held
The sharpest-sighted spi'rit of all in heav'n;
Who to the fraudulent impostor foul
In his uprightness answer thus returned:]
Fair angel, thy desire which tends to know   III.694
The works of God, thereby to glorify
The great Work-Master, leads to no excess
That reaches blame, but rather merits praise
The more it seems excess, that led thee hither
From thy empyreal mansion thus alone,
To witness with thine eyes what some perhaps   III.700
Contented with report hear only' in heav'n:
For wonderful indeed are all his works,
Pleasant to know, and worthiest to be all
Had in remembrance always with delight.
But what created mind can comprehend   III.705
Their number, or the wisdom infinite
That brought them forth, but hid their causes deep?
I saw when at his word the formless mass,
This world's material mould, came to a heap:
Confusion heard his voice, and wild uproar   III.710

Stood ruled, stood vast infinitude confined;
Till at his second bidding darkness fled,
Light shone, and order from disorder sprung.
Swift to their sev'ral quarters hasted then
The cumbrous elements, earth, flood, air, fire.   III.715
And this ethereal quintessence of heav'n
Flew upward, spirited with various forms,
That rolled orbicular, and turned to stars
Numberless, as thou seest, and how they move;
Each had his place appointed, each his course;   III.720
The rest in circuit walls this universe.
Look downward on that globe, whose hither side
With light from hence, though but reflected, shines;
That place is Earth, the seat of Man, that light
His day, which else as th'other hemisphere   III.725
Night would invade; but there the neighb'ring moon
(So call that opposite fair star) her aid
Timely' interposes, and her monthly round
Still ending, still renewing, through mid-heav'n,
With borrowed light, her countenance triform   III.730
Hence fills and empties to enlighten th'earth,
And in her pale dominion checks the night.
That spot to which I point is Paradise,
Adam's abode, those lofty shades his bow'r.
Thy way thou canst not miss, me mine requires . . .   III.735

Notes on Book III

1. *A drop serene* – either a *qutta serena*, or *suffusion*, is a species of blindness which is generally incurable.
2. *Irradiate* – shine into, enlighten.
3. *My umpire* – to arbitrate between them and me.
4. They *extolled thee*, turning *back*.
5. A *tiara* is a kind of coronet.
6. *Cogitation* – thought.

BOOK IV

The Argument

Satan now, in prospect of Eden, and nigh the place where he must now attempt the bold enterprise which he undertook alone against God and man, falls into many doubts with himself, and many passions, fear, envy, and despair; but at length confirms himself in evil, journeys on to Paradise, whose outward prospect and situation is described; overleaps the bounds, sits in the shape of a cormorant on the tree of life, as highest in the garden, to look about him. The garden described; Satan's first sight of Adam and Eve; his wonder at their excellent form and happy state, but with resolution to work their fall; overhears their discourse, thence gathers that the tree of knowledge was forbidden them to eat of, under penalty of death; and thereon intends to found his temptation, by seducing them to transgress: then leaves them awhile, to know further of their state by some other means. Meanwhile Uriel, descending on a sunbeam, warns Gabriel, who had in charge the gate of Paradise, that some evil spirit had escaped the deep, and passed at noon by his sphere in the shape of a good angel, down to Paradise, discovered after by his furious gestures in the mount. Gabriel promises to find him ere morning. Night coming on, Adam and Eve discourse of going to their rest: their bower described; their evening worship. Gabriel drawing forth his bands of night-watch to walk the round of Paradise, appoints two strong angels to Adam's bower, lest the evil spirit should be there doing some harm to Adam or Eve sleeping; there they find him at the ear of Eve, tempting her in a dream, and bring him, though unwilling, to Gabriel: by whom questioned, he scornfully answers, prepares resistance, but hindered by a sign from heaven flies out of Paradise.

[[Satan], much revolving, thus in sighs began:]   IV.31
  O thou that with surpassing glory crowned
Look'st from thy sole dominion like the God
Of this new world; at whose sight all the stars
Hide their diminished heads; to thee I call,
But with no friendly voice, and add thy name,
O Sun, to tell thee how I hate thy beams,
That bring to my remembrance from what state
I fell, how glorious once above thy sphere;
Till pride and worse ambition threw me down,   IV.40
Warring in heav'n against heav'n's matchless king.
Ah wherefore? He deserved no such return
From me, whom he created what I was
In that bright eminence, and with his good
Upbraided none; nor was his service hard.   IV.45
What could be less than to afford him praise,
The easiest recompence, and pay him thanks,
How due! Yet all his good proved ill in me,
And wrought but malice; lifted up so high
I 'sdained[1] subjection, and thought one step higher   IV.50
Would set me highest, and in a moment quit
The debt immense of endless gratitude,
So burdensome, still paying, still to owe:
Forgetful what from him I still received,
And understood not that a grateful mind   IV.55
By owing owes not, but still pays, at once
Indebted and discharged; what burden then?
O had his pow'rful destiny ordained
Me some inferior angel, I had stood
Then happy; no unbounded hope had raised   IV.60
Ambition. Yet why not? Some other pow'r as great
As great might have aspired, and me, though mean,
Drawn to his part; but other pow'rs as great
Fell not, but stand unshaken, from within
Or from without, to all temptations armed.   IV.65
Hadst thou the same free will and pow'r to stand?
Thou hadst: whom hast thou then or what to' accuse,
But heav'n's free love dealt equally to all?
Be then his love accursed, since love or hate,
To me alike, it deals eternal woe.   IV.70

Nay, cursed be thou; since against his thy will
Chose freely what it now so justly rues.
Me miserable! Which way shall I fly
Infinite wrath, and infinite despair?
Which way I fly is hell; myself am hell;   IV.75
And in the lowest deep a lower deep
Still threat'ning to devour me opens wide,
To which the hell I suffer seems a heav'n.
O then at last relent: is there no place
Left for repentance, none for pardon left?   IV.80
None left but by submission; and that word
Disdain forbids me, and my dread of shame
Among the spi'rits beneath, whom I seduced
With other promises and other vaunts
Than to submit, boasting I could subdue   IV.85
Th'Omnipotent. Ah me, they little know
How dearly I abide that boast so vain,
Under what torments inwardly I groan,
While they adore me on the throne of hell.
With diadem and sceptre high advanced,   IV.90
The lower still I fall, only supreme
In misery; such joy ambition finds!
But say I could repent, and could obtain
By act of grace my former state; how soon
Would height recall high thoughts, how soon unsay   IV.95
What feigned submission swore? Ease would recant
Vows made in pain, as violent and void.
For never can true reconcilement grow,
Where wounds of deadly hate have pierced so deep;
Which would but lead me to a worse relapse   IV.100
And heavier fall: so should I purchase dear
Short intermission bought with double smart.
This knows my punisher; therefore as far
From granting he, as I from begging peace.
All hope excluded thus, behold instead   IV.105
Of us outcast, exiled, his new delight,
Mankind created, and for him this world.
So farewell hope, and with hope farewell fear,
Farewell remorse. All good to me is lost;
Evil, be thou my good; by thee at least   IV.110

Divided empire with heav'n's king I hold,
By thee, and more than half perhaps will reign;
As man ere long, and this new world shall know . . .   IV.113
[So on he fares, and to the border comes]   IV.131
Of Eden, where delicious Paradise,
Now nearer, crowns with her enclosure green,
As with a rural mound,[2] the champain head
Of a steep wilderness, whose hairy sides   IV.135
With thicket overgrown, grotesque[3] and wild,
Access denied; and overhead up-grew
Insuperable height of loftiest shade,
Cedar, and pine, and fir, and branching palm,
A sylvan scene, and as the ranks ascend   IV.140
Shade above shade, a woody theatre
Of stateliest view. Yet higher than their tops
The verd'rous wall of Paradise up-sprung:
Which to our gen'ral sire gave prospect large
Into his nether empire neighb'ring round.[4]   IV.145
And higher than that wall a circling row
Of goodliest trees loaden with fairest fruit,
Blossoms and fruit at once, of golden hue,
Appeared, with gay enamelled colours mixed:
On which the sun more glad impressed his beams   IV.150
Than on fair ev'ning cloud, or humid bow,[5]
When God hath showered the earth; so lovely seemed
That landskip; and of pure now purer air
Meets his approach, and to the heart inspires
Vernal delight and joy, able to drive   IV.155
All sadness but despair. Now gentle gales,
Fanning their odoriferous[6] wings, dispense
Native perfumes[7] . . . And now to th'ascent   IV.158,172
Satan had journeyed on, pensive and slow . . .   IV.173
Beneath him with new wonder now he views,   IV.205
To all delight of human sense exposed,
In narrow room nature's whole wealth, yea more,
A heav'n on earth; for blissful Paradise
Of God the garden was, by him in th'east
Of Eden planted; Eden stretched her line   IV.210
From Auran eastward to the royal tow'rs
Of great Seleucia . . . in this pleasant soil   IV.212,214

His far more pleasant garden God ordained;
Out of the fertile ground he caused to grow
All trees of noblest kind for sight, smell, taste;
And all amid them stood the tree of life,
High eminent, blooming ambrosial fruit
Of vegetable gold; and next to life,   IV.220
Our death, the tree of knowledge, grew fast by,
Knowledge of good, bought dear by knowing ill.   IV.222
[Southward through Eden went a river large . . .
And country, whereof here needs no account;]   IV.235
But rather to tell how, if art could tell,
How from that sapphire fount the crisped[8] brooks,
Rolling on orient[9] pearl, and sands of gold,
With mazy error under pendent shades
Ran nectar,[10] visiting each plant, and fed   IV.240
Flow'rs worthy of Paradise, which not nice art
In beds and curious knots, but nature boon[11]
Poured forth profuse, on hill, and dale, and plain,
Both where the morning sun first warmly smote
The open field, and where the unpierced shade   IV.245
Imbrowned the noontide bow'rs. Thus was this place
A happy rural seat of various view . . . Yet here the fiend
                                                    IV.247,285
Saw undelighted all delight, all kind
Of living creatures new to sight, and strange.
Two of far nobler shape, erect and tall,
Godlike erect, with native honour clad
In naked majesty, seemed lords of all,   IV.290
And worthy seemed; for in their looks divine
The image of their glorious Maker shone,
Truth, wisdom, sanctitude severe and pure
(Severe,[12] but in true filial freedom placed).
Whence true authority in men; though both   IV.295
Not equal, as their sex not equal seemed;
For contemplation he and valour formed,
For softness she and sweet attractive grace;
He for God only, she for God in him:
His fair large front and eye sublime declared   IV.300
Absolute rule; and hyacinthine[13] locks
Round from his parted forelock manly hung

Clust'ring, but not beneath his shoulders broad:
She as a veil down to the slender waist
Her unadorned golden tresses wore   IV.305
Dishevelled, but in wanton ringlets waved
As the vine curls her tendrils, which implied
Subjection,[14] but required with gentle sway . . .   IV.308
[When Satan, still in gaze as first he stood,   IV.356
Scarce thus at length failed speech recovered sad:]
    O hell! What do mine eyes with grief behold!
Into our room of bliss thus high advanced
Creatures of other mould, earth-born perhaps,   IV.360
Not spirits, yet to heav'nly spirits bright
Little inferior; whom my thoughts pursue
With wonder, and could love, so lively shines
In them divine resemblance, and such grace
The hand that formed them on their shape hath poured.   IV.365
Ah gentle pair, ye little think how nigh
Your change approaches, when all these delights
Will vanish, and deliver you to woe,
More woe, the more your taste is now of joy;
Happy, but for so happy ill secured   IV.370
Long to continue, and this high seat your heav'n
Ill fenced for heav'n to keep out such a foe
As now is entered; yet no purposed foe
To you, whom I could pity thus forlorn,
Though I unpitied. League with you I seek,   IV.375
And mutual amity so strait, so close,
That I with you must dwell, or you with me
Henceforth; my dwelling haply may not please,
Like this fair Paradise, your sense, yet such
Accept your Maker's work; he gave it me,   IV.380
Which I as freely give. Hell shall unfold,
To entertain you two, her widest gates,
And send forth all her kings; there will be room,
Not like these narrow limits, to receive
Your num'rous offspring; if no better place,   IV.385
Thank him who puts me, loath, to this revenge
On you, who wrong me not, for him who wronged.
And should I at your harmless innocence
Melt, as I do, yet public reason just,

Honour and empire with revenge enlarged,   IV.390
By conqu'ring this new world, compels me not
To do what else, though damned, I should abhor.
    So spake the fiend, and with necessity,
The tyrant's plea, excused his devilish deeds . . .   IV.394
           [. . . Adam, first of men,
To first of women, Eve, thus moving speech,
Turned him all ear to hear new utt'rance flow:]   IV.410
    Sole partner, and sole part[15] of all these joys,
Dearer thyself than all; needs must the Pow'r
That made us, and for us this ample world,
Be infinitely good, and of his good
As liberal and free as infinite;   IV.415
That raised us from the dust, and placed us here
In all this happiness, who at his hand
Have nothing merited, nor can perform
Aught whereof he hath need, he who requires
From us no other service than to keep   IV.420
This one, this easy charge, of all the trees
In Paradise that bear delicious fruit
So various, not to taste that only tree . . .   IV.423
    To whom thus Eve replied. O thou for whom   IV.440
And from whom I was formed, flesh of thy flesh,
And without whom am to no end, my guide
And head, what thou hast said is just and right.
For we to him indeed all praises owe,
And daily thanks; I chiefly who enjoy   IV.445
So far the happier lot, enjoying thee
Pre-eminent by so much odds, while thou
Like consort to thyself canst nowhere find.
That day I oft remember, when from sleep
I first awaked, and found myself reposed   IV.450
Under a shade, on flow'rs, much wond'ring where
And what I was, whence thither brought, and how.
Not distant far from thence a murm'ring sound
Of water issued from a cave, and spread
Into a liquid plain, then stood unmoved,   IV.455
Pure as th'expanse of heav'n; I thither went
With unexperienced thought, and laid me down
On the green bank, to look into the clear

Smooth lake, that to me seemed another sky.
As I bent down to look, just opposite   IV.460
A shape within the wat'ry gleam appeared,
Bending to look on me. I started back,
It started back; but pleased I soon returned;
Pleased it returned as soon with answ'ring looks
Of sympathy and love. There I had fixed   IV.465
Mine eyes till now, and pined with vain desire,
Had not a voice thus warned me, What thou seest,
What there thou seest, fair creature, is thyself;
With thee it came and goes: but follow me,
And I will bring thee where no shadow stays   IV.470
Thy coming, and thy soft embraces – he
Whose image thou art; him thou shalt enjoy
Inseparably thine; to him shalt bear
Multitudes like thyself, and thence be called
Mother of human race. What could I do,   IV.475
But follow straight, invisibly thus led?
Till I espied thee, fair indeed and tall,
Under a plantane;[16] yet methought less fair,
Less winning soft, less amiably mild,
Than that smooth wat'ry image. Back I turned;   IV.480
Thou following criedst aloud, Return, fair Eve;
Whom fliest thou? Whom thou fliest, of him thou art,
His flesh, his bone; to give thee being I lent
Out of my side to thee, nearest my heart,
Substantial life, to have thee by my side   IV.485
Henceforth an individual solace dear:
Part of my soul I seek thee, and thee claim
My other half. With that thy gentle hand
Seized mine; I yielded, and from that time see
How beauty is excelled by manly grace   IV.490
And wisdom, which alone is truly fair.
    So spake our gen'ral mother, and with eyes
Of conjugal attraction unreproved,
And meek surrender, half embracing leaned
On our first father; half her swelling breast   IV.495
Naked met his under the flowing gold
Of her loose tresses hid: he in delight,
Both of her beauty, and submissive charms,

Smiled with superior love . . . and pressed her lip   IV.499.501
With kisses pure. Aside the devil turned
For envy, yet with jealous leer malign
Eyed them askance, and to himself thus plained: IV.504
  [Sight hateful, sight tormenting! Thus these two
Imparadised in one another's arms,
The happier Eden, shall enjoy their fill
Of bliss on bliss; while I to hell am thrust . . .]   IV.508
Yet let me not forget what I have gained   IV.512
From their own mouths: all is not theirs, it seems;
One fatal tree there stands, of knowledge called,
Forbidden them to taste: Knowledge forbidden! . . .
Yet happy pair, enjoy, till I return,   IV.534
Short pleasures, for long woes are to succeed . . .

Uriel reports to Gabriel that Satan has been in Paradise

  [He spake; and Uriel to the sun returned,]   IV.589–91
Arraying with reflected purple and gold   IV.596
The clouds that on his western throne attend.
Now came still ev'ning on, and twilight grey
Had in her sober liv'ry all things clad;
Silence accompanied; for beast and bird,   IV.600
They to their grassy couch, these to their nests
Were slunk, all but the wakeful nightingale;
She all night long her am'rous descant sung;
Silence was pleased: now glowed the firmament
With living sapphires; Hesperus,[17] that led   IV.605
The starry host, rode brightest, till the moon,
Rising in clouded majesty, at length
Apparent queen unveiled her peerless light,
And o'er the dark her silver mantle threw.
  When Adam thus to Eve: Fair consort, th'hour   IV.610
Of night, and all things now retired to rest,
Mind us of like repose, since God hath set
Labour and rest, as day and night, to men
Successive; and the timely dew of sleep
Now falling, with soft slumb'rous weight inclines   IV.615
Our eyelids. Other creatures all day long
Rove idle unemployed, and less need rest;
Man hath his daily work of body or mind

Appointed, which declares his dignity,
And the regard of heav'n on all his ways;   IV.620
While other animals unactive range,
And of their doings God takes no account . . .   IV.622
  To whom thus Eve, with perfect beauty adorned: IV.634
My author and disposer, what thou bidst
Unargued I obey; so God ordains . . .   IV.636
With thee conversing, I forget all time;   IV.639
All seasons, and their change, all please alike.
Sweet is the breath of morn, her rising sweet,
With charm of earliest birds; pleasant the sun,
When first on this delightful land he spread
His orient[18] beams, on herb, tree, fruit, and flow'r,
Glitt'ring with dew: fragrant the fertile earth   IV.645
After soft show'rs; and sweet the coming on
Of grateful ev'ning mild; then silent night,
With this her solemn bird, and this fair moon,
And these, the gems of heav'n, her starry train:
But neither breath of morn, when she ascends,   IV.650
With charm of earliest birds; nor rising sun
On this delightful land; nor herb, fruit, flow'r,
Glist'ring with dew; nor fragrance after show'rs;
Nor grateful ev'ning mild; nor silent night,
With this her solemn bird, nor walk by moon,   IV.655
Or glitt'ring starlight, without thee is sweet . . .   IV.657
  [To whom our gen'ral ancestor replied: IV.659
Daughter of God and man, accomplished Eve,
These have their course to finish round the earth . . .]   IV.661
Then not in vain; nor think, though men were none,   IV.675
That heav'n would want spectators, God want praise.
Millions of spiritual creatures walk the earth
Unseen, both when we wake, and when we sleep:
All these with ceaseless praise his works behold
Both day and night . . .   IV.680
  [Thus talking, hand in hand alone they passed   IV.689
On to their blissful bow'r . . . Each beauteous flow'r,] IV.690,697
Iris all hues, roses, and jessamine,   IV.698
Reared high their flourished heads between, and wrought
Mosaic;[19] under foot the violet,
Crocus, and hyacinth, with rich inlay

Broidered the ground, more coloured than with stone
Of costliest emblem . . .   IV.703
   Thus at their shady lodge arrived, both stood,   IV.720
Both turned, and under open sky adored
The God that made both sky, air, earth, and heav'n,
Which they beheld, the moon's resplendent globe,
And starry pole: Thou also mad'st the night,
Maker omnipotent, and thou the day,   IV.725
Which we in our appointed work employed
Have finished, happy in our mutual help,
And mutual love, the crown of all our bliss . . .   IV.728
Hail, wedded love, mysterious law,[20] true source   IV.750
Of human offspring, sole propriety
In Paradise of all things common else.
By thee adult'rous lust was driv'n from men
Among the bestial herds to range; by thee,
Founded in reason, royal, just, and pure.   IV.755
Relations dear, and all the charities[21]
Of father, son, and brother first were known.
Far be it that I should write thee sin or blame,
Or think thee unbefitting holiest place,
Perpetual fountain of domestic sweets,   IV.760
Whose bed is undefiled and chaste pronounced,
Present, or past, as saints or patriarchs used.
Here love his golden shafts employs, here lights
His constant lamp, and waves his purple wings,
Reigns here and revels; not in the bought smile   IV.765
Of harlots, loveless, joyless, unendeared,
Casual fruition; nor in court amours,
Mixed dance, or wanton mask, or midnight ball,
Or serenade,[22] which the starved lover sings
To his proud fair, best quitted with disdain . . .   IV.770
   [Ithuriel and Zephon, with wing speed   IV.788
Search through this garden, leave unsearched no nook . . .
In search of whom they sought; him there they found,
Squat like a toad, close at the ear of Eve . . .]   IV.800
Him thus Ithuriel with his spear   IV.810
Touched lightly; for no falsehood can endure
Touch of celestial temper,[23] but returns
Of force to its own likeness. Up he starts,

Discovered and surprised. As when a spark
Lights on a heap of nitrous powder, laid   IV.815
Fit for the tun, some magazine to store
Against a rumoured war, the smutty grain
With sudden blaze diffused inflames the air;
So started up in his own shape the fiend.
Back stepped those two fair angels, half amazed
So sudden to behold the grisly king;
Yet thus, unmoved with fear, accost him soon . . .   IV.822
[So spake the Cherub; and his grave rebuke,]   IV.844
Severe in youthful beauty, added grace
Invincible. Abashed the devil stood,
And felt how awful goodness is, and saw
Virtue in her shape how lovely; saw, and pined
His loss; but chiefly to find here observed
His lustre visible impaired . . .   IV.850
      The fiend replied not, overcome with rage;   IV.857
But like a proud steed reined, went haughty on,
Champing his iron curb: to strive or fly
He held it vain: awe from above had quelled
His heart, not else dismayed . . .   IV.861
      [Gabriel from the front thus called aloud . . .   IV.865
Why hast thou, Satan, broke the bounds prescribed   IV.878
To thy transgressions . . . ?
      [To whom thus Satan with contemptuous brow: IV.885
Gabriel, thou hadst in heav'n th'esteem of wise,
And such I held thee; but this question asked
Puts me in doubt.] Lives there who loves his pain? . . .   IV.888
      While thus he spake, th'angelic squadron bright   IV.977
Turned fiery red, sharp'ning in mooned horns
Their phalanx,[24] and began to hem him round
With ported spears,[25] as thick as when a field   IV.980
Of Ceres[26] ripe for harvest waving bends
Her bearded grove of ears, which way the wind
Sways them . . . On th'other side Satan, alarmed,   IV.983,985
Collecting all his might, dilated stood,
Like Teneriffe[27] or Atlas unremoved:
His stature reached the sky, and on his crest
Sat horror plumed; nor wanted in his grasp
What seemed both spear and shield. Now dreadful deeds   IV.990

Might have ensued, nor only Paradise
In this commotion, but the starry cope
Of heav'n perhaps, or all the elements
At least had gone to wreck, disturbed and torn
With violence of this conflict, had not soon   IV.995
Th'Eternal to prevent such horrid fray
Hung forth in heav'n his golden scales,[28] yet seen
Betwixt Astrea and the Scorpion sign,
Wherein all things created first he weighed,
The pendulous round earth with balanced air,   IV.1000
In counterpoise, now ponders all events,
Battles and realms. In these he put two weights,
The sequel each of parting and of fight:
The latter quick up-flew, and kicked the beam;
Which Gabriel spying, thus bespake the fiend.   IV.1005
Satan, I know thy strength, and thou know'st mine,
Neither our own but giv'n; what folly then
To boast what arms can do! Since thine no more
Than heav'n permits, nor mine, though doubled now
To trample thee as mire. For proof look up,   IV.1010
And read thy lot in yon celestial sign,
Where thou art weighed, and shown how light, how weak,
If thou resist. The fiend looked up, and knew
His mounted scale aloft: nor more; but fled
Murm'ring, and with him fled the shades of night.   IV.1015

Notes on Book IV

1. *'sdained* – disdained.
2. *A rural mound* – Such a fence as is used in the country; *champain* – even, level.
3. *Grotesque* – irregular.
4. *His nether empire neighbouring round* – beginning at the foot of the Mount of Paradise.
5. *Humid bow* – the rainbow.
6. *Odoriferous* – bringing sweet smells.
7. *Native perfumes* – not made by art.
8. *Crisped* – curling, winding.
9. *Orient* – beautiful.
10. *Ran nectar* – delicious, as the nectar which the poets feigned to be the drink of the gods.
11. *Boon* – good, bountiful

12. *Severe* – exact, strict.

13. *Hyacinthine* – raven-black.

14. *Implied subjection* – of which a veil was the token.

15. *Sole part* – that part of them which alone is dearer than all the rest.

16. *Plantane* – a plane-tree, a very broad-leaved tree.

17. *Hesperus* – the evening star, Venus.

18. *Orient* – rising.

19. *Mosaic* pavement is chequered with small inlaid stones, of various colours.

20. *Mysterious law* – containing a deep meaning, which few understand.

21. *Charities* – love, tenderness, endearments.

22. *Serenade* – a song sung at night by a lover under the window of his mistress.

23. *Of celestial temper* – of the spear which was tempered in heaven.

24. A *phalanx* is a square body of soldiers drawn up close together.

25. *Ported spears* held sloping toward the enemy.

26. *Ceres* – corn.

27. *Teneriffe* is one of the highest mountains in the world.

28. *His golden scales.* Libra, or *the scales*, is one of the twelve signs through which the sun moves yearly, between *Astrea* (or *Virgo*) and the *Scorpion*. This also alludes to the word spoken to Belshazzar, 'Thou art weighed in the balance and found wanting.'

BOOK V

The Argument

Morning approaches; Eve relates to Adam her troublesome dream.
He likes it not, yet comforts her. They come forth to their day
labours: their morning hymn at the door of their bower. God sends
Raphael to admonish man of his obedience, of his free estate, of his
enemy near at hand, who he is, and why his enemy, and whatever
else may avail Adam to know. Raphael comes down to Paradise. His
appearance described; his coming discerned by Adam afar off, sitting
at the door of his bower. He goes out to meet him, brings him to his
lodge, entertains him with the choicest fruits of Paradise, got together
by Eve. Their discourse at table. Raphael performs his message;
minds Adam of his state, and of his enemy; relates, at Adam's request,
who that enemy is, and how he came to be so, beginning from his
first revolt in heaven, and the occasion thereof: how he drew his
legions after him to the parts of the north, and there enticed them to
rebel with him, persuading all but only Abdiel, a seraph; who, in
argument, dissuades and opposes him, then forsakes him.

[His wonder was to find unwakened Eve,   V.9
With tresses discomposed and glowing cheek,]
As through unquiet rest: he on his side
Leaning half raised, with looks of cordial love
Hung over her enamoured, and beheld
Beauty, which whether waking, or asleep,
Shot forth peculiar graces: then with voice   V.15
Mild, as when Zephyrus on Flora breathes,
Her hand soft touching, whispered thus: Awake,
My fairest, my espoused, my latest found,
Heav'n's last best gift, my ever new delight.
Awake; the morning shines, and the fresh field   V.20

Calls us; we lose the prime, to mark how spring
Our tended plants, how blows the citron grove,
What drops the myrrh, and what the balmy reed,
How nature paints her colours, how the bee
Sits on the bloom extracting liquid sweet . . .   V.25
Why sleep'st thou, Eve? Now is the pleasant time,   V.38
The cool, the silent, save where silence yields
To the night-warbling bird, that now awake,
Tunes sweetest his love-laboured song; now reigns
Full orbed the moon, and with more pleasing light,
Shadowy sets off the face of things; in vain,
If none regard: heav'n wakes with all his eyes;
Whom to behold but thee, nature's desire?   V.45
In whose sight all things joy, with ravishment
Attracted by thy beauty still to gaze . . .   V.47
   So cheered he his fair spouse, and she was cheered,   V.129
But silently a gentle tear let fall
From either eye, and wiped them with her hair;
Two other precious drops that ready stood,
Each in their crystal sluice, he, ere they fell,
Kissed, as the gracious signs of sweet remorse
And pious awe, that feared to have offended . . .   V.135
   [Lowly they bowed adoring, and began   V.144
Their orisons, each morning duly paid . . .]   V.145
These are thy glorious works, Parent of good,   V.153
Almighty, thine this universal frame,
Thus wond'rous fair; thyself how wond'rous then!
To us invisible, or dimly seen
In these thy lowest works; yet these declare
Thy goodness beyond thought, and pow'r divine.
Speak ye who best can tell, ye sons of light,   V.160
Angels; for ye behold him, and with songs
And choral symphonies, day without night,
Circle his throne rejoicing; ye in heav'n:
On earth join all ye creatures to extol
Him first, him last, him midst, and without end.   V.165
Fairest of stars, last in the train of night,
If better thou belong not to the dawn,
Sure pledge of day, that crown'st the smiling morn
With thy bright circlet, praise him in thy sphere,

While day arises, that sweet hour of prime.   V.170
Thou sun, of this great world both eye and soul,
Acknowledge him thy greater, sound his praise
In thy eternal course, both when thou climb'st,
And when high noon hast gained, and when thou fall'st.
Moon, that now meet'st the orient sun, now fly'st . . .   V.175
And ye five other wand'ring fires[1] that move   V.177
In mystic dance, not without song,[2] resound
His praise, who out of darkness called up light.
Air, and ye elements, the eldest birth   V.180
Of nature's womb, that in quaternion[3] run
Perpetual circle, multiform;[4] and mix
And nourish all things; let your ceaseless change
Vary to our great Maker still new praise.
Ye mists and exhalations that now rise   V.185
From hill or steaming lake, dusky or gray,
Till the sun paint your fleecy skirts with gold,
In honour to the world's great Author rise,
Whether to deck with clouds th'uncoloured sky,
Or wet the thirsty earth with falling showers,   V.190
Rising or falling still advance his praise.
His praise ye winds, that from four quarters blow,
Breathe soft or loud; and wave your tops, ye pines,
With every plant, in sign of worship wave.
Fountains, and ye that warble as ye flow,   V.195
Melodious murmurs, warbling tune his praise.
Join voices, all ye living souls. Ye birds,
That singing up to heaven's gate ascend,
Bear on your wings and in your notes his praise.
Ye that in waters glide, and ye that walk   V.200
The earth, and stately tread, or lowly creep,
Witness if *I* be silent, morn or even,
To hill, or valley, fountain or fresh shade
Made vocal by my song, and taught his praise.
Hail, universal Lord, be bounteous still   V.205
To give us only good; and if the night
Have gathered aught of evil, or concealed,
Disperse it, as now light dispels the dark . . .   V.208

Raphael is sent to Paradise

At once on th'eastern cliff of Paradise   V.275
He lights, and to his proper shape returns,[5]
A seraph winged; six wings he wore, to shade
His lineaments divine; the pair that clad
Each shoulder broad, came mantling o'er his breast
With regal ornament; the middle pair   V.280
Girt like a starry zone[6] his waist, and round
Skirted his loins and thighs with downy gold
And colours dipped in heav'n; the third his feet
Shadowed from either heel with feathered mail,[7]
Sky-tinctured grain. Like Maia's son[8] he stood,
And shook his plumes, that heav'nly fragrance filled
The circuit wide. . . .   V.287

Raphael cautions Adam

God made thee perfect, not immutable;   V.524
And good he made thee, but to persevere
He left it in thy pow'r; ordained thy will
By nature free, not over-ruled by fate
Inextricable,[9] or strict necessity:
Our voluntary service he requires,
Not our necessitated. Such with him   V.530
Finds no acceptance, nor can find; for how
Can hearts, not free, be tried whether they serve
Willing or no, who will but what they must? . . .   V.533
Myself, and all the'angelic host, that stand   V.535
In sight of God enthroned, our happy state
Hold, as you yours, while our obedience holds;
On other surety none; freely we serve,
Because we freely love, as in our will
To love or not; in this we stand or fall . . .   V.540

Abdiel accuses Satan of blasphemy.

He said, and as the sound of waters deep   V.872
Hoarse murmur echoed to his words applause
Through the infinite host. Nor less for that
The flaming seraph fearless, though alone,
Encompassed round with foes, thus answered bold . . .   V.876
[That golden sceptre which thou didst reject   V.886

Is now an iron rod to bruise and break
Thy disobedience . . .   V.888
     So spake the seraph Abdiel, faithful found.]   V.896
Among the faithless, faithful only he;
Among innumerable false, unmoved,
Unshaken, unseduced, unterrified,
His loyalty he kept, his love, his zeal;   V.900
Nor number, nor example with him wrought
To swerve from truth, or change his constant mind,
Though single.   V.903

Notes on Book V

1. *Wand'ring fires* – planets.
2. *Not without song*. The music of the spheres was much talked of among the ancient philosophers.
3. *In quaternion* – fourfold.
4. *Multiform* – in many forms.
5. *To his proper shape returns*. He stood on his feet, and replaced his wings in their proper situation.
6. *Zone* – a girdle.
7. *With feathered mail* – one feather coming a little short of the other, like the plates on a coat of mail.
8. *Maia's son* – Mercury, supposed by the heathens to be the messenger of Jupiter, and pictured with wings at his feet.
9. *Inextricable* – from which none can extricate or free himself.

BOOK VI

The Argument

Raphael continues to relate how Michael and Gabriel were sent forth to battle against Satan and his angels. The first fight described: Satan and his powers retire under night; he calls a council, invents devilish engines, which in the second day's fight put Michael and his angels to some disorder; but they at length, pulling up mountains, overwhelmed both the force and machines of Satan. Yet the tumult not so ending, God on the third day sends Messiah his Son, for whom he had reserved the glory of that victory. He, in the power of his Father, coming to the place, and causing all his legions to stand still on either side, with his chariot and thunder driving into the midst of his enemies, pursues them, unable to resist, towards the wall of heaven; which opening, they leap down with horror and confusion into the place of punishment prepared for them in the deep. Messiah returns with triumph to his Father.

There is a cave	VI.4
Within the mount of God, fast by his throne,	
Where light and darkness in perpetual round	
Lodge and dislodge by turns, which makes through heaven	
Grateful vicissitude, like day and night;	
Light issues forth, and at the other door	
Obsequious darkness enters, till her hour	VI.10
To veil the heav'n, though darkness there might well	
Seem twilight here. And now went forth the morn,	
Such as in highest heav'n . . .	VI.13

Abdiel's courage is praised

Servant of God, well done! Well hast thou fought	VI.29
The better fight, who single hast maintained	
Against revolted multitudes the cause	

Of truth, in word mightier than they in arms;
And for the testimony of truth hast borne
Universal reproach, far worse to bear
Than violence; for this was all thy care,
To stand approved in sight of God, though worlds
Judged thee perverse . . .   VI.37

Abdiel challenges and attacks Satan

All are not of thy train; there be who faith   VI.142
Prefer, and piety to God, though then
To thee not visible when I alone
Seemed in thy world erroneous to dissent
From all. My sect thou seest; now learn too late
How few sometimes may know, when thousands err . . . VI.148
    So saying, a noble stroke he lifted high,   VI.189
Which hung not, but so swift with tempest fell
On the proud crest of Satan, that no sight,
Nor motion of swift thought, less could his shield
Such ruin intercept: ten paces huge
He back recoiled; the tenth on bended knee
His massy spear upstayed. As if on earth   VI.195
Winds underground, or waters forcing way,
Sidelong had pushed a mountain from his seat,
Half sunk with all his pines . . . Dire was the noise   V.198,211
Of conflict; overhead the dismal hiss
Of fiery darts in flaming volleys flew,
And flying vaulted either host with fire.
So under fiery cope together rushed   VI.215
Both battles main with ruinous assault
And inextinguishable rage; all heaven
Resounded, and had earth been then, all earth
Had to her centre shook. What wonder, when
Millions of fierce encount'ring angels fought   VI.220
On either side, the least of whom could wield
These elements, and arm him with the force
Of all their regions: how much more of power
Army against army numberless to raise
Dreadful combustion warring, and disturb,   VI.225
Though not destroy, their happy native seat;
Had not th'eternal King omnipotent

From his stronghold of heav'n, high overruled
And limited their might; though in number such
As each divided legion might have seemed   VI.230
A numerous host, in strength each armed hand
A legion. Led in fight, yet leader seemed
Each warrior single as in chief; expert
When to advance, or stand, or turn the sway
Of battle, open when, and when to close
The ridges[1] of grim war . . . Satan . . . at length   VI.236.246,249
Saw where the sword of Michael smote, and felled
Squadrons at once; with huge two-handed sway
Brandished aloft the horrid edge came down
Wide-wasting. Such destruction to withstand
He hasted, and opposed the rocky orb
Of tenfold adamant, his ample shield,
A vast circumference . . .   VI.256
Now waved their fiery swords, and in the air   VI.304
Made horrid circles; two broad suns their shields
Blazed opposite, while expectation stood
In horror; from each hand with speed retired,
Where erst was thickest fight, th'angelic throng,
And left large field, unsafe within the wind
Of such commotion; such as, to set forth   VI.310
Great things by small, if, nature's concord broke,
Among the constellations war were sprung,
Two planets rushing from aspect malign
Of fiercest opposition in mid sky
Should combat, and their jarring spheres confound. VI.315
Together both next to almighty arm
Uplifted imminent; one stroke they aimed
That might determine, and not need repeat,
As not of pow'r at once. Nor odds appeared
In might or swift prevention: but the sword   VI.320
Of Michael from the armoury of God
Was giv'n him tempered so that neither keen
Nor solid might resist that edge: it met
The sword of Satan with steep force to smite
Descending, and in half cut sheer; not stayed,   VI.325
But with swift wheel reverse, deep ent'ring shared[2]
All his right side: then Satan first knew pain,

And writhed him to and fro convolved;³ so sore
The griding⁴ sword with discontinuous⁵ wound
Passed through him; but th'ethereal substance closed,   VI.330
Not long divisible; and from the gash
A stream of nect'rous humour issuing flowed
Sanguine, such as celestial Spi'rits may bleed,
And all his armour stained, erewhile so bright . . .   VI.334
Yet soon he healed; for spi'rits that live throughout   VI.344
Vital in every part, not as frail man
In entrails, heart, or head, liver or reins,
Cannot but by annihilating die;
Nor in their liquid⁶ texture mortal wound
Receive, no more than can the fluid air:
All heart they live, all head, all eye, all ear,   VI.350
All intellect, all sense; and as they please
They limb themselves, and colour, shape, or size
Assume, as likes them best, condense or rare . . .   VI.354

  Satan's supporters complain

                            For what avails   VI.456
Valour or strength, though matchless, quelled with pain
Which all subdues, and makes remiss the hands
Of mightiest? Sense of pleasure we may well
Spare out of life, perhaps, and not repine . . .   VI.460
But pain is perfect misery, the worst   VI.462
Of evils, and excessive, overturns
All patience . . .   VI.464

  The angels frustrate Satan's devices on the second day

Forthwith (behold the excellence, the power,   VI.637
Which God hath in his mighty angels placed)
Their arms away they threw, and to the hills
(For earth hath this variety from heaven   VI.640
Of pleasure situate in hill and dale)
Light as the lightning glimpse they ran, they slew.
From their foundations, loos'ning to and fro,
They plucked the seated hills with all their load,
Rocks, waters, woods, and by the shaggy tops   VI.645
Uplifting, bore them in their hands. Amaze,
Be sure, and terror seized the rebel host,
When coming towards them so dread they saw

The bottom of the mountains upward turned;
Till on those cursed engines triple-row   VI.650
They saw them whelmed, and all their confidence
Under the weight of mountains buried deep;
Themselves invaded next, and on their heads
Main promontories flung, which in the air
Came shadowing, and oppressed whole legions armed;   VI.655
Their armour helped their harm, crushed in and bruised
Into their substance pent, which wrought them pain
Implacable, and many a dolorous groan,
Long struggling underneath, ere they could wind
Out of such prison, though spi'rits of purest light,   VI.660
Purest at first, now gross by sinning grown.
The rest in imitation to like arms
Betook them, and the neighb'ring hills uptore;
So hills amid the air encountered hills,
Hurled to and fro with jaculation⁷ dire,
That underground they fought in dismal shade . . .   VI.666

On the third day Messiah joins the heavenly host

    Forth rushed with whirlwind sound   VI.749
The chariot of paternal Deity,
Flashing thick flames, wheel within wheel undrawn,
Itself instinct with spirit, but convoyed
By four cherubic shapes; four faces each
Had, wondrous; as with stars their bodies all
And wings were set with eyes, with eyes the wheels   VI.755
Of beryl,⁸ and careering fires between;⁹
Over their heads a crystal firmament,
Whereon a sapphire throne, inlaid with pure
Amber, and colours of the show'ry arch.
He, in celestial panoply all armed   VI.760
Of radiant Urim,¹⁰ work divinely wrought,
Ascended; at his right hand victory
Sat eagle-winged; beside him hung his bow
And quiver with three-bolted thunder stored,
And from about him fierce effusion rolled   VI.765
Of smoke and bickering flame¹¹ and sparkles dire.
Attended with ten thousand thousand [saints],
He onward came; far off his coming shone;

And twenty thousand (I their number heard)
Chariots of God, half on each hand were seen.　　VI.770
He on the wings of cherub rode sublime
On the crystalline sky, in sapphire throned,
Illustrious far and wide, but by his own
First seen; them unexpected joy surprised,
When the great ensign of Messiah blazed
Aloft by angels borne, his sign in heaven . . .　　VI.776
Before him pow'r divine his way prepared.　　VI.780
At his command th'uprooted hills retired
Each to his place; they heard his voice, and went
Obsequious; heav'n his wonted face renewed,
And with fresh flow'rets hill and valley smiled . . .　　VI.784
　　　[The great Son of God　　VI.799
To all his host on either hand thus spake:
Stand still in bright array, ye saints, here stand,
Ye angels armed, this day from battle rest.
Faithful hath been your warfare, and of God
Accepted, fearless in his righteous cause.
And as ye have received, so have ye done,
Invincibly; but of this cursed crew
The punishment to other hand belongs . . .]　　VI.807
　　So spake the Son, and into terror changed　　VI.824
His count'nance, too severe to be beheld,
And full of wrath bent on his enemies.
At once the four spread out their starry wings
With dreadful shade contiguous, and the orbs
Of his fierce chariot rolled, as with the sound
Of torrent floods, or of a numerous host.　　VI.830
He on his impious foes right onward drove,
Gloomy as night; under his burning wheels
The steadfast empyrean shook throughout,
All but the throne itself of God. Full soon
Among them he arrived, in his right hand　　VI.835
Grasping ten thousand thunders, which he sent
Before him, such as in their souls infixed
Plagues. They, astonished, all resistance lost,
All courage; down their idle weapons dropped.
Over shields and helms and helmed heads he rode　　VI.840
Of thrones and mighty seraphim prostrate,

That wished the mountains now might be again
Thrown on them as a shelter from his ire.
Nor less on either side tempestuous fell
His arrows, from the fourfold-visaged four,   VI.845
Distinct with eyes, and from the living wheels,
Distinct alike with multitude of eyes;
One spirit in them ruled, and every eye
Glared lightning, and shot forth pernicious fire
Among th'accurs'd, that withered all their strength,   VI.850
And of their wonted vigour left them drained,
Exhausted, spiritless, afflicted, fall'n.
Yet half his strength he put not forth, but checked
His thunder in mid-volley; for he meant
Not to destroy, but root them out of heaven . . .   VI.855
   Hell heard th'unsufferable noise, hell saw   VI.867
Heav'n ruining from heav'n, and would have fled
Affrighted; but strict fate had cast too deep
Her dark foundations, and too fast had bound.   VI.870
Nine days they fell; confounded Chaos roared,
And felt tenfold confusion in their fall
Through his wild anarchy, so huge a rout
Encumbered him with ruin: hell at last
Yawning received them whole, and on them closed;   VI.875
Hell their fit habitation, fraught with fire
Unquenchable, the house of woe and pain.

Notes on Book VI

1. *The ridges.* The ranks are figuratively so called, alluding to a ploughed field.

2. *Shared* – pierced through.

3. *Convolved* – bowed together.

4. *Griding* – to *gride* is to cut.

5. *Discontinuous* – dividing the parts from each other.

6. *Liquid* – pliable, flexible, not solid or hard.

7. *Jaculation* – darting, tossing.

8. *Beryl* is a precious stone of a sea green colour.

9. *And careering fires between* – striking forward, whirling, slashing: lightnings, darting out straight, then turning quick every way.

10. *Urim* – light.

11. *Bickering flame* – breaking out in sudden flashes, and kindling it to fury, Ezek. 1.4. It is a *fire enfolding itself*, literally, *fire catching itself*.

BOOK VII

The Argument

Raphael, at the request of Adam, relates how and wherefore this world was first created; that God, after the expelling of Satan and his angels out of heaven, declared his pleasure to create another world, and other creatures to dwell therein; sends his Son with glory and attendance of angels to perform the work of creation in six days; the angels celebrate with hymns the performance thereof, and his reascension into heaven.

Adam asks Raphael to explain the beginnings of the world

How first began this heav'n which we behold	VII.86
Distant so high, with moving fires adorned	
Innumerable, and this which yields or fills	
All space, the ambient air wide interfused[1]	
Embracing round this florid earth? . . .	VII.90
And the great light of day yet wants to run	VII.98
Much of his race, though steep. Suspense in heaven,	
Held by thy voice, thy potent voice he hears,	
And long will delay to hear thee tell	
His generation, and the rising birth	
Of nature from the unapparent deep.	
Or if the star of evening and the moon	
Haste to thy audience, night with her will bring	VII.105
Silence, and sleep, list'ning to thee, will watch,	
Or we can bid his absence, till thy song	
End, and dismiss thee ere the morning shine.	VII.108
[Thus Adam his illustrious guest besought;	VII.109
And thus the godlike angel answered mild.]	
This also thy request, with caution asked,	VII.111
Obtain: though to recount Almighty works	

What words or tongue of seraph can suffice,
Or heart of man suffice to comprehend?
Yet what thou canst attain, which best may serve
To glorify the Maker, and infer
Thee also happier, shall not be withheld . . .]   VII.117
But knowledge is as food, and needs no less   VII.126
Her temp'rance over appetite, to know
In measure what the mind may well contain;
Oppresses else with surfeit, and soon turns
Wisdom to folly, as nourishment to wind . . .   VII.130

Raphael describes God's charge to 'His Word, the Filial Godhead' (175),
and the rejoicing in heaven that he was to replace the fallen angels by
bringing 'a better race' (189) to Earth

So sang the hierarchies. Meanwhile the Son   VII.192
On his great expedition now appeared,
Girt with omnipotence, with radiance crowned
Of majesty divine, sapience[2] and love
Immense, and all his Father in him shone.
About his chariot numberless were poured
Cherubim, and seraph, potentates and thrones,
And virtues, winged spirits, and chariots winged
From th'armoury of God, where stand of old   VII.200
Myriads between two brazen mountains lodged[3]
Against a solemn day, harnessed at hand,
Celestial equipage; and now came forth
Spontaneous, for within them spirit lived,
Attendant on their Lord; heav'n opened wide   VII.205
Her ever-during gates, harmonious sound
On golden hinges moving, to let forth
The King of Glory, in his pow'rful Word
And Spirit coming to create new worlds.
On heav'nly ground they stood, and from the shore   VII.210
They viewed the vast immeasurable abyss
Outrageous as a sea, dark, wasteful, wild,
Up from the bottom turned by furious winds
And surging waves, as mountains, to assault
Heav'n's height, and with the centre mix the pole.   VII.215
Silence, ye troubled waves, and thou deep, peace,
Said then th'omnific[4] Word, your discord end.

Nor stayed, but on the wings of cherubim
Uplifted, in paternal glory rode
Far into Chaos, and the world unborn;   VII.220
For Chaos heard his voice: him all his train
Followed in bright procession to behold
Creation, and the wonders of his might.
Then stayed the fervid wheels, and in his hand
He took the golden compasses, prepared   VII.225
In God's eternal store, to circumscribe
This universe, and all created things.
One foot he centred, and the other turned
Round through the vast profundity obscure,
And said, Thus far extend, thus far thy bounds,
This be thy just circumference, O world . . .   VII.231
    Let there be light, said God, and forthwith light   VII.243
Ethereal, first of things, quintessence pure
Sprung from the deep, and from her native east
To journey through the aery gloom began,
Sphered in a radiant cloud, for yet the sun
Was not; she in a cloudy tabernacle
Sojourned the while. [God saw the light was good;
And light from darkness by the hemisphere   VII.250
Divided:⁵ light the day, and darkness night
He named.] Thus was the first day ev'n and morn;
Nor passed uncelebrated, nor unsung
By the celestial choirs, when orient light
Exhaling first from darkness they beheld,
Birthday of heav'n and earth. With joy and shout
The hollow universal orb they filled . . .   VII.257
    [Again God said, Let there be firmament . . .] VII.261
Immediately the mountains huge appear   VII.285
Emergent, and their broad bare backs upheave
Into the clouds, their tops ascend the sky:
So high as heaved the tumid hills, so low
Down sunk a hollow bottom broad and deep,
Capacious bed of waters . . .   VII.290
All but within those banks where rivers now   VII.305
Stream, and perpetual draw their humid train. VII.306
[The dry land, earth, and the great receptacle   VII.307
Of congregated waters he called seas;

And saw that it was good, and said, Let th'earth
Put forth the verdant grass . . .   VII.310
He scarce had said, when the bare earth, till then   VII.313
Desert and bare, unsightly, unadorned,]
Brought forth the tender grass, whose verdure clad   VII.315
Her universal face with pleasant green;
Then herbs[6] of every leaf, that sudden flow'red,
Opening their various colours, and made gay
Her bosom, smelling sweet; and these scarce blown,
Forth flourished thick the clust'ring vine, forth crept   VII.320
The swelling gourd, up stood the corny[7] reed
Embattled in her field, and th'humble shrub,
And bush with frizzled hair implicit;[8] last
Rose as in dance the stately trees, and spread
Their branches hung with copious fruit, or gemmed[9]   VII.325
Their blossoms. With high woods the hills were crowned,
With tufts the valleys and each fountain side,
With borders long the rivers, that earth now
Seemed like to heav'n, a seat where gods might dwell . . . VII.329
Of the celestial bodies first the sun   VII.354
A mighty sphere he framed, unlightsome first,
Though of ethereal mould; then formed the moon
Globose, and eve'ry magnitude of stars,
And sowed with stars the heav'n thick as a field.
Of light by far the greater part he took,
Transplanted from her cloudy shrine, and placed   VII.360
In the sun's orb, made porous to receive
And drink the liquid light, firm to retain
Her gathered beams, great palace now of light.
Hither as to their fountain other stars
Repairing, in their golden urns draw light,
And hence the morning planet[10] gilds her horns . . .   VII.366
First in his east the glorious lamp was seen,   VII.370
Regent of day, and all th'horizon round
Invested with bright rays, jocund to run
His longitude[11] through heav'n's high road; the gray
Dawn, and the Pleiades[12] before him danced,
Shedding sweet influence. Less bright the moon,   VII.375
But opposite in levelled west, was set,
Her mirror, with full face borrowing her light

From him, for other light she needed none
In that aspect, and still that distance keeps
Till night, then in the east shines . . . and her reign   VII.380,381
With thousand lesser lights divided holds . . .   VII.382
  [And God said, Let the waters generate . . .   VII.387
Forthwith the sounds and seas, each creek and bay   VII.399
With fry innumerable swarm, and shoals]
Of fishes that with fins and shining scales   VII.401
Glide under the green wave, in sculls[13] that oft
Bank the mid sea. Part, single or with mate,
Graze the seaweed, their pasture, and through groves
Of coral stray, or sporting with quick glance
Show to the sun their waved coats dropped with gold . . .   VII.406
       . . . The swan, with arched neck   VII.438
Between her white wings mantling proudly, rows
Her state with oary feet; yet oft they quit
The dank, and rising on stiff pennons, tower
The mid aereal sky. Others on ground
Walked firm; the crested cock, whose clarion sounds
The silent hours, and th'other[14], whose gay train
Adorns him, coloured with the florid hue
Of rainbows and starry eyes . . .   VII.446
   The grassy clods now calved;[15] now half appeared   VII.463
The tawny lion, pawing to get free
His hinder parts, then springs as broke from bands,
And rampant shakes his brinded mane; the ounce,[16]
The libbard, and the tiger, as the mole
Rising, the crumbled earth above them threw
In hillocks; the swift stag from underground
Bore up his branching head . . .   VII.470
[At once came forth whatever creeps the ground,]   VII.475
Insect or worm. Those waved their limber fans
For wings, and smallest lineaments exact
In all the liveries decked of summer's pride,
With spots of gold and purple, azure and green;
These as a line their long dimensions drew,   VII.480
Streaking the ground with sinuous[17] trace; not at all
Minims of nature; some of serpent kind,
Wondrous in length and corpulence, involved
Their snaky folds, and added wings . . .   VII.484

Now heav'n in all her glory shone, and rolled   VII.499
Her motions as the great First Mover's hand
First wheeled their course; earth in her rich attire
Consummate lovely smiled . . .   VII.502

Notes on Book VII

1. *Interfused* – insinuating into and betwixt all other bodies.
2. *Sapience* – wisdom.
3. The thought is taken from Zech. 6:1.
4. *Omnific* – all-creating.
5. *By the hemisphere divided* – one half of the globe being enlightened, the other not.
6. *Then* the earth brought forth *herbs*.
7. *Corny* – stiff like horn.
8. *Implicit* – entangled.
9. *Gemmed* – budded forth.
10. *The morning planet*, Venus, varies her appearances, just as the moon does.
11. *His longitude* – his course from East to West.
12. *The Pleiades* – the Seven Stars.
13. *Sculls* – shoals so large as to appear like banks in the sea.
14. *Th'other* – the peacock.
15. *Calved* – brought forth.
16. *The ounce* – more usually termed lynx.
17. *Sinuous* – winding.

BOOK VIII

The Argument

Adam inquires concerning celestial motions, is doubtfully answered, and exhorted to search rather things more worthy of knowledge. Adam assents, and still desirous to detain Raphael, relates to him what he remembered since his own creation, his placing in Paradise, his talk with God concerning solitude and fit society, his first meeting and nuptials with Eve, his discourse with the angel thereupon; who after admonitions repeated departs.

Raphael replies to Adam's questions about God's government of the universe

But whether thus these things, or whether not,	VIII.159
Whether the sun predominant in heaven	
Rise on the earth, or earth rise on the sun,	
He from the east his flaming road begin,	
Or from the west her silent course advance	
With inoffensive pace that spinning sleeps	
On her soft axle, while she paces even,	VIII.165
And bears thee soft with the smooth air along,	
Solicit not thy thoughts with matters hid:	
Leave them to God above, him serve and fear.	
Of other creatures, as him pleases best,	
Wherever placed, let him dispose. Joy thou	
In what he gives to thee, this Paradise	
And thy fair Eve; heav'n is for thee too high	
To know what passes there; be lowly wise . . .	VIII.173
[To whom thus Adam, cleared of doubt, replied:]	VIII.179
While I sit with thee, I seem in heaven,	VIII.210
And sweeter thy discourse is to my ear	
Than fruit of palm tree pleasantest to thirst	
And hunger both, from labour, at the hour	
Of sweet repast; they satiate, and soon fill,	

Though pleasant; but thy words, with grace divine
Imbued, bring to their sweetness no satiety . . .   VIII.216

Adam describes his creation

   For man to tell how human life began   VIII.250
Is hard; for who himself beginning knew?
Desire with thee still longer to converse
Induced me. As new waked from soundest sleep,
Soft on the flow'ry herb I found me laid
In balmy sweat, which with his beams the sun   VIII.255
Soon dried, and on the reeking moisture fed.
Straight toward heav'n my wond'ring eyes I turned,
And gazed awhile the ample sky, till raised
By quick instinctive motion up I sprung,
As thitherward endeavouring, and upright   VIII.260
Stood on my feet; about me round I saw
Hill, dale, and shady woods, and sunny plains,
And liquid lapse of murm'ring streams; by these,
Creatures that lived and moved and walked, or flew,
Birds on the branches: all things smiled   VIII.265
With fragrance; and with joy my heart o'erflowed.
Myself I then perused, and limb by limb
Surveyed, and sometimes went, and sometimes ran
With supple joints, as lively vigour led:
But who I was, or where, or from what cause,   VIII.270
Knew not. To speak I tried, and forthwith spake;
My tongue obeyed, and readily could name
Whate'er I saw. Thou sun, said I, fair light,
And thou enlightened earth, so fresh and gay,
Ye hills, and dales, ye rivers, woods, and plains,   VIII.275
And ye that live and move, fair creatures, tell,
Tell, if ye saw, how came I thus, how here?
Not of myself; by some great Maker then,
In goodness and in power pre-eminent.
Tell me how may I know him, how adore,   VIII.280
From whom I have that thus I move and live,
And feel that I am happier than I know.
While thus I called, and strayed I knew not whither
From where I first drew air, and first beheld
This happy light, when answer none returned,   VIII.285

On a green shady bank profuse of flowers,
Pensive I sat me down. There gentle sleep
First found me, and with soft oppression seized
My drowsed sense, untroubled, though I thought
I was then passing to my former state   VIII.290
Insensible, and forthwith to dissolve.
When suddenly stood at my head a dream,
Whose inward apparition gently moved
My fancy to believe I yet had being,
And lived. One came, methought, of shape divine   VIII.295
And said, Thy mansion wants thee, Adam, rise,
First man. of men innumerably ordained
First father, called by thee I come thy guide
To the garden of bliss, thy seat prepared.
So saying, by the hand he took me, raised,   VIII.300
And over fields and waters, as in air
Smooth sliding without step, last led me up
A woody mountain; whose high top was plain,
A circuit wide, enclosed, with goodliest trees
Planted, with walks, and bow'rs, that what I saw   VIII.305
Of earth before scarce pleasant seemed. Each tree
Loaden with fairest fruit, that hung to th'eye
Tempting, stirred in me sudden appetite
To pluck and eat. Whereat I waked, and found
Before mine eyes all real, as the dream   VIII.310
Had lively shadowed. Here had new begun
My wand'ring, had not he who was my guide
Up hither, from among the trees appeared,
Presence divine . . .   VIII.314

God appears before Adam, asking him to name his creatures

As thus he spake, each bird and beast behold   VIII.349
Approaching two and two, these cow'ring[1] low
With blandishment,[2] each bird stooped on his wing.
I named them as they passed, and understood
Their nature, with such knowledge God endued
My sudden apprehension. But in these
I found not what methought I wanted still,   VIII.355
[And to the heavenly vision thus presumed . . .   VIII.356
Thou hast provided all things: but with me   VIII.363

I see not who partakes. In solitude
What happiness? . . . The vision . . . thus replied:

VIII.365,367,368

With these find pastime, and bear rule . . .   VIII.374,375
I with leave of speech implored . . .   VIII.377
Hast thou not made me here thy substitute,   VIII.381
And these inferior far beneath me set?
Among unequals what society
Can sort, what harmony or true delight? . . .   VIII.384
Thus I emboldened spake, and freedom used   VIII.434
Permissive, and acceptance found . . .]   VIII.435
Mine eyes he closed, but open left the cell   VIII.460
Of fancy, my internal sight, by which
Abstract[3] as in a trance methought I saw,
Though sleeping, where I lay, I saw the shape
Still glorious before whom awake I stood;
Who, stooping opened my left side, and took   VIII.465
From thence a rib, with cordial spirits warm,
And life-blood streaming fresh. Wide was the wound,
But suddenly with flesh filled up and healed.
The rib he formed and fashioned with his hands;
Under his forming hands a creature grew,   VIII.470
Manlike, but different sex, so lovely fair,
That what seemed fair in all the world seemed now
Mean, or in her summed up, in her contained
And in her looks, which from that time infused
Sweetness into my heart, unfelt before.   VIII.475
[She disappeared, and left me dark. I waked
To find her, or for ever to deplore
Her loss, and other pleasures all abjure.
When out of hope, behold her, not far off,   VIII.480
Such as I saw her in my dream, adorned
With what all earth or heaven could bestow]
To make her amiable. On she came,
Led by her heav'nly Maker, though unseen,
And guided by his voice, nor uninformed   VIII.485
Of nuptial sanctity and marriage rites.
Grace was in all her steps, heaven in her eye,
In every gesture dignity and love.   VIII.488
[I overjoyed could not forbear aloud . . .

I now see   VIII.494
Bone of my bone, flesh of my flesh, myself
Before me. Woman is her name, of Man
Extracted; for this cause he shall forego
Father and mother, and to his wife adhere;
And they shall be one flesh, one heart, one soul.]   VIII.499
   She heard me thus, and though divinely brought,   VIII.500
Yet innocence and virgin modesty,
Her virtue and the conscience⁴ of her worth,
That would be wooed, and not unsought be won,
Not obvious⁵, nor obtrusive,⁶ but retired,⁷
The more desirable, or to say all,   VIII.505
Nature herself, though pure of sinful thoughts,
Wrought in her so, that seeing me, she turned.
I followed her; she what was honour knew,
And with obsequious⁸ majesty approved
My pleaded reason. To the nuptial bower   VIII.510
I led her blushing like the morn. All heaven,
And happy constellations on that hour
Shed their selectest influence; the earth
Gave sign of gratulation, and each hill;
Joyous the birds; fresh gales and gentle airs   VIII.515
Whispered it to the woods, and from their wings
Flung rose, flung odours from the spicy shrub,
Disporting, till the amorous bird of night
Sung spousal, and bid haste the evening star
On this hill top, to light the bridal lamp.   VIII.520
   [⁹Thus have I told thee all my state, and brought
My story to the sum of earthly bliss
Which I enjoy, and must confess to find
In all things else, indeed, but such
As used or not works in the mind no change   VIII.525
Nor vehement desire; these delicacies
I mean of taste, sight, smell, herbs, fruits, and flowers,
Walks, and the melody of birds; but here
Far otherwise, transported I behold,
Transported touch; here passion first I felt,   VIII.530
Commotion strange, in all enjoyments else
Superior and unmoved, here only weak
Against the charm of beauty's pow'rful glance . . .   VIII.533

For well I understand in the prime end   VIII.540
Of nature her th'inferior, in the mind
And inward faculties, which most excel;
In outward also her resembling less
His image who made both, and less expressing
The character of that dominion given]   VIII.545
O'er other creatures; yet when I approach
Her loveliness, so absolute she seems,
And in herself complete, so well to know
Her own, that what she wills to do or say,
Seems wisest, virtuousest, discreetest, best;   VIII.550
All higher knowledge in her presence falls
Degraded, wisdom in discourse with her
Loses discount'nanced, and like folly shows . . .   VIII.553
Greatness of mind and nobleness their seat   VIII.557
Build in her loveliest, and create an awe
About her, as a guard angelic placed.   VIII.559
   [To whom the angel, with contracted brow: VIII.560
. . . Nature hath done her part; do thou but thine. . . .
                                                           VIII.561,562
For what admir'st thou, what transports thee so?   VIII.567
An outside? Fair, no doubt, and worthy well
Thy cherishing, thy honouring, and thy love,
Not thy subjection. Weigh with her thyself,]   VIII.570
Then value. Oft-times nothing profits more   VIII.571
Than self-esteem, grounded on just and right,
Well managed; of that skill the more thou know'st
The more she will acknowledge thee her head,
And to realities yields all her shows.
Made so adorned for thy delight the more,
So aweful, that with honour thou may'st love
Thy mate, who sees when thou art seen least wise . . .   VIII.578
What higher in her society thou find'st   VIII.586
Attractive, human, rational, love still;
In loving thou dost well, in passion not,
Wherein true love consists not. Love refines
The thoughts, and heart enlarges, hath his seat
In reason, and is judicious, is the scale
By which to heav'nly love thou may'st ascend . . .   VIII.592
   To whom thus half abashed Adam replied: VIII.595

Neither her outside formed so fair, nor aught
In procreation common to all kinds
(Though higher of the genial bed by far,
And with mysterious reverence I deem)
So much delights me, as those graceful acts,　　　　VIII.600
Those thousand decencies that daily flow
From all her words and actions, mixed with love
And sweet compliance, which declare unfeigned
Union of mind, or in us both one soul;
(Harmony to behold in wedded pair) . . .　　　　VIII.605
[To whom the angel with a smile that glowed . . .]　　VIII.618
Whatever pure thou in the body enjoy'st　　　　VIII.622
(And pure thou wert created) we enjoy
In eminence, and obstacle find none
Of membrane, joint, or limb, exclusive bars;
Easier than air with air, if sp'rits embrace,
Total they mix, union of pure with pure . . .　　　　VIII.627

Notes on Book VIII

1. *Cow'ring* – bending, bowing themselves.
2. *Blandishment* – making court.
3. *Abstract* – abstracted from the body.
4. *Conscience* – consciousness.
5. *Obvious* – forward.
6. *Obtrusive* – thrusting herself on me.
7. *Retired* – modest, backward.
8. *Obsequious* – yielding, obedient.
9. [It seems likely that an asterisk was here omitted from Wesley's text by error, at the opening of this new section on the status and character of women, and of married love; certainly his printer placed an asterisk at VIII.546, which was thus mistakenly shown as a new paragraph. Similarly there was an asterisk at the end of VIII.559 which might well have been intended by Wesley for the beginning of VIII.560.]

BOOK IX

The Argument

Satan, having compassed the earth, with meditated guile returns as a mist by night into Paradise, enters into the serpent, sleeping. Adam and Eve in the morning go forth to their labours, which Eve proposes to divide in several places, each labouring apart. Adam consents not, alleging the danger, lest that enemy, of whom they were forewarned, should attempt her, found alone. Eve, loath to be thought not circumspect or firm enough, urges her going apart, the rather desirous to make trial of her strength; Adam at last yields. The serpent finds her alone; his subtle approach, first gazing, then speaking, with much flattery extolling Eve above all other creatures. Eve, wondering to hear the serpent speak, asks how he attained to human speech and such understanding; the serpent answers, that by tasting of a certain tree in the garden he attained both to speech and reason, till then void of both. Eve requires him to bring her to that tree, and finds it to be the tree of knowledge forbidden. The serpent now grows bolder, with many wiles and arguments induces her at length to eat; she, pleased with the taste, deliberates awhile whether to impart thereof to Adam or not, at last brings him of the fruit, relates what persuaded her to eat thereof. Adam, at first amazed, but perceiving her lost, resolves through vehemence of love to perish with her; and extenuating the trespass eats also of the fruit. The effects thereof in them both; they seek to cover their nakedness; then fall to variance and accusation of one another.

Satan, close to Paradise, ponders his journey round the Earth

[O earth, how like to heav'n, if not preferred! . . .]   IX.98
With what delight could I have walked thee round,   IX.114
If I could joy in aught, sweet interchange
Of hill, and valley, rivers, woods, and plains,

Now land, now sea, and shores with forest crowned,
Rocks, dens, and caves! But I in none of these
Find place or refuge; and the more I see
Pleasures about me, so much more I feel   IX.120
Torment within; all good to me becomes
Bane, and in heav'n much worse would be my state.
But neither here seek I, no, nor in heaven
To dwell, unless by mast'ring heav'n's supreme;
Nor hope to be myself less miserable
By what I see, but others to make such
As I, though thereby worse to me redound . . .   IX.128
O foul descent! That I who erst contended   IX.163
With gods to sit the high'st, am now constrained
Into a beast, and mixed with bestial slime,
This essence to incarnate and imbrute,
That to the height of deity aspired.
But what will not ambition and revenge
Descend to? Who aspires must down as low
As high he soared, obnoxious first or last
To basest things. Revenge, at first though sweet,
Bitter ere long back on itself recoils . . .   IX.172

Eve suggests to Adam that they work apart; he replies:

[Well hast thou motioned, well thy thoughts employed   IX.229
How we might best fulfil the work which here
God hath assigned us, nor of me shalt pass]
Unpraised: for nothing lovelier can be found
In woman than to study household good,
And good works in her husband to promote.
Yet not so strictly hath our Lord imposed   IX.235
Labour as to debar us when we need
Refreshment, whether food, or talk between,
Food of the mind, or this sweet intercourse
Of looks and smiles, for smiles from reason flow,
To brute denied, and are of love the food –   IX.240
Love, not the lowest end of human life.
For not to irksome toil, but to delight
He made us, and delight to reason joined . . .   IX.243
[But if much converse perhaps   IX.247
Thee satiate, to short absence I could yield;]

For solitude sometimes is best society,
And short retirement urges sweet return . . .   IX.250
I from the influence of thy looks receive   IX.309
Access[1] in every virtue, in thy sight
More wise, more watchful, stronger, if need were
Of outward strength; while shame, thou looking on,
Shame to be overcome or over-reached
Would utmost vigour raise, and raised unite.
Why shouldst not thou like sense within thee feel
When I am present, and thy trial choose
With me, best witness of thy virtue tried?   IX.317
     [So spake domestic Adam in his care   IX.318
And matrimonial love; but Eve, who thought
Less attributed to her faith sincere,
Thus her reply with accent sweet renewed:
If this be our condition, thus to dwell
In narrow circuit straitened by a foe . . .   IX.323
How are we happy, still in fear of harm? . . .   IX.326
Let us not then suspect our happy state   IX.337
Left so imperfect by the Maker wise,
As not secure to single or combined.
Frail is our happiness if this be so,
And Eden were no Eden thus exposed.]   IX.341
     To whom thus Adam fervently replied: IX.342
O woman, best are all things as the will
Of God ordained them; his creating hand
Nothing imperfect or deficient left
Of all that he created, much less Man,
Or aught that might his happy state secure,
Secure from outward force; within himself
The danger lies, yet lies within his power:
Against his will he can receive no harm.   IX.350
But God left free the will, for what obeys
Reason is free, and reason he made right;
But bid her well beware,[2] and still erect,[3]
Lest by some fair appearing good surprised,
She dictate false, and misinform the will
To do what God expressly hath forbid . . .   IX.356
[So spake the patriarch of mankind; but Eve   IX.376
Persisted; yet submiss, though last, replied:

With thy permission, then, and thus forewarned . . .   IX.378
The willinger I go, nor much expect   IX.382
A foe so proud will first the weaker seek . . .]   IX.383
Her long with ardent look his eye pursued,   IX.397
Delighted, but desiring more her stay.
Oft he to her his charge of quick return
Repeated, she to him as oft engaged   IX.400
To be returned by noon amid the bower,
And all things in best order to invite
Noontide repast, or afternoon's repose.
O much deceived, much failing, hapless Eve! . . .   IX.404
Thou never from that hour in Paradise   IX.406
Found either sweet repast or sound repose . . .   IX.407
[Much pleasure took the serpent to behold]   IX.455
This flo'ry plat, the sweet recess of Eve,
Thus early, thus alone; her heav'nly form
Angelic, but more soft, and feminine,
Her graceful innocence, her every air
Of gesture or least action overawed   IX.460
His malice, and with rapine sweet, bereaved
His fierceness of the fierce intent it brought.
That space the evil one abstracted stood
From his own evil, and for the time remained
Stupidly good, of enmity disarmed,   IX.465
Of guile, of hate, of envy, of revenge.
But the hot hell that always in him burns,
Though in mid heav'n, soon ended his delight,
And tortures him now more, the more he sees
Of pleasure not for him ordained . . .   IX.470
[The enemy of mankind . . . in serpent . . . toward Eve]
    IX.494,495
Addressed his way, not with indented wave,   IX.496
Prone on the ground, as since, but on his rear,
Circular base of rising folds, that towered,
Fold above fold a surging maze, his head
Crested aloft, and carbuncle[4] his eyes;
With burnished neck of verdant gold, erect
Amidst his circling spires . . .   IX.502
[His fraudulent temptation thus began:]   IX.531
    Wonder not, sov'reign mistress, if perhaps   IX.532

Thou canst, who art sole wonder; much less arm
Thy looks, the heav'n of mildness, with disdain,
Displeased that I approach thee thus, and gaze   IX.535
Insatiate, I thus single, nor have feared
Thy awful brow, more awful thus retired.
Fairest resemblance of thy Maker fair,
Thee all things living gaze on, all things thine
By gift, and thy celestial beauty adore,   IX.540
With ravishment beheld, there best beheld
Where universally admired. But here,
In this enclosure wild, these beasts among,
Beholders rude, and shallow to discern
Half what in thee is fair, one man except,   IX.545
Who sees thee? (And what is one?) Who shouldst be seen,
A goddess among gods, adored and served
By angels numberless, thy daily train . . .   IX.548

   Being tempted, Eve ate the forbidden fruit

Earth felt the wound, and nature from her seat   IX.782
Sighing through all her works gave signs of woe,
That all was lost . . .   IX.784

   Eve wonders how she should approach Adam

  But to Adam in what sort   IX.816
Shall I appear? Shall I to him make known
As yet my change, and give him to partake
Full happiness with me, or rather not,
But keep the odds of knowledge in my pow'r   IX.820
Without copartner? So to add what wants
In female sex, the more to draw his love,
And render me more equal, and perhaps,
A thing not undesirable, sometime
Superior; for inferior who is free?   IX.825
This may be well; but what if God have seen,
And death ensue? Then I shall be no more,
And Adam wedded to another Eve,
Shall live with her enjoying, I extinct;
A death to think. Confirmed then I resolve   IX.830
Adam shall share with me in bliss or woe:
So dear I love him, that with him all deaths

I could endure, without him live no life . . .   IX.833

Informed of her sin, Adam resolves to die with her

However, I with thee have fixed my lot,   IX.952
Certain to undergo like doom; if death
Consort with thee[5], death is to me as life;   IX.954
So forcible within my heart I feel
The bond of nature draw me to my own,
My own in thee, for what thou art is mine.
Our state cannot be severed, we are one,
One flesh; to lose thee were to lose myself.

    So Adam, and thus Eve to him replied: IX.960
O glorious trial of exceeding love,
Illustrious evidence, example high!
Engaging me to emulate, but short
Of thy perfection, how shall I attain,
Adam? From whose dear side I boast me sprung,   IX.965
And gladly of our union hear thee speak,
One heart, one soul in both; whereof good proof
This day affords, declaring thee resolved,
Rather than death or aught than death more dread
Shall separate us, linked in love so dear,   IX.970
To undergo with me one guilt, one crime,
If any be, of tasting this fair fruit,
Whose virtue (for of good still good proceeds
Direct, or by occasion) hath presented
This happy trial of thy love, which else   IX.975
So eminently, never had been known.
Were it I thought death menaced would ensue
This my attempt, I would sustain alone
The worst, and not persuade thee. Rather die
Deserted, than oblige thee with a fact   IX.980
Pernicious to thy peace, chiefly assured
Remarkably so late of thy so true,
So faithful love unequalled. But I feel
Far otherwise th'event, not death, but life
Augmented, opened eyes, new hopes, new joys,   IX.985
Taste so divine, that what of sweet before
Hath touched my sense, flat seems to this, and harsh.
On my experience, Adam, freely taste,

And fear of death deliver to the winds.
  So saying, she embraced him, and for joy   IX.990
Tenderly wept, much won that he his love
Had so ennobled, as of choice to incur
Divine displeasure for her sake, or death.
In recompense (for such compliance bad
Such recompense best merits) from the bough   IX.995
She gave him of that fair enticing fruit
With liberal hand. He scrupled not to eat,
Against his better knowledge, not deceived,
But fondly overcome with female charm.
Earth trembled from her entrails as again   IX.1000
In pangs, and nature gave a second groan,
Sky loured, and muttering thunder, some sad drops
Wept at completing of the mortal sin
Original . . .   IX.1004

In shame, Adam laments

             [O might I here   IX.1086
In solitude live savage, in some glade]
Obscured, where highest woods impenetrable
To star or sunlight, spread their umbrage[6] broad
And brown as evening. Cover me, ye pines,
Ye cedars, with innumerable boughs
Hid me, where I may never see them more . . .   IX.1090
[Would thou hadst hearkened to my words, and stayed] IX.1134
With me, as I besought thee, when that strange
Desire of wand'ring this unhappy morn,
I know not whence, possessed thee; we had then
Remained still happy, not as now, despoiled
Of all our good, shamed, naked, miserable.
Let none henceforth seek needless cause t'approve
The faith they owe; when earnestly they seek
Such proof, conclude, they then begin to fail . . . IX.1142

Notes on Book IX

1. *Access* – increase.
2. *Beware* – wary.
3. *Erect* – on its guard.

4. *Carbuncle* – fiery red, like a carbuncle.
5. *If death consort with thee* – attend thee; if thou must die.
6. *Umbrage* – shade.

BOOK X

The Argument

Man's transgression known, the guardian angels forsake Paradise, and return up to heaven to approve their vigilance, and are approved, God declaring that the entrance of Satan could not be by them prevented. He sends his Son to judge the transgressors, who descends and gives sentence accordingly; then in pity clothes them both, and reascends. Sin and Death sitting till then at the gates of hell, by wondrous sympathy feeling the success of Satan in this new world, and the sin by man there committed, resolve to sit no longer confined in hell, but to follow Satan their sire up to the place of man. To make the way easier from hell to this world to and fro, they pave a broad highway or bridge over Chaos, according to the track that Satan first made; then preparing for Earth, they meet him proud of his success returning to hell; their mutual gratulation. Satan arrives at Pandemonium, in full assembly relates with boasting his success against man; instead of applause is entertained with a general hiss by all his audience, transformed with himself also suddenly into serpents, according to his doom given in Paradise; then deluded with a show of the forbidden tree springing up before them, they greedily reaching to take of the fruit, chew dust and bitter ashes. The proceedings of Sin and Death; God foretells the final victory of his Son over them, and the renewing of all things; but for the present commands his angels to make several alterations in the heavens and elements. Adam more and more perceiving his fallen condition, heavily bewails, rejects the condolement of Eve; she persists, and at length appeases him. Then, to evade the curse likely to fall on their offspring, proposes to Adam violent ways, which he approves not, but conceiving better hope, puts her in mind of the late promise made them, that her seed should be revenged on the Serpent, and exhorts her with him to seek peace of the offended deity, by repentance and supplication.

The sentence of God on man, conveyed by his Son

So judged he man, both Judge and Saviour sent,   X.209
And th'instant stroke of death denounced that day
Removed far off; then, pitying how they stood
Before him naked to the air, that now
Must suffer changed, disdained not to begin
Thenceforth the form of servant to assume,
As when he washed his servants' feet, so now . . .   X.215
He clad their nakedness with skins of beasts.   X.216,217

Death speaks to his father Sin

So saying, with delight he snuffed the smell   X.272
Of mortal change on earth. As when a flock
Of ravenous fowl, though many a league remote,
Against the day of battle, to a field
Where armies lie encamped come flying, lured
With scent of living carcases designed
For death the following day, in bloody fight;
So scented the grim feature, and upturned
His nostril wide into the murky air,   X.280
Sagacious of his quarry from so far.
Then both from out hell gates into the waste
Wide anarch of Chaos, damp and dark,
Flew diverse, and with pow'r (their pow'r was great)
Hovering upon the waters, what they met
Solid or slimy, as in raging sea
Tossed up and down, together crowded drove
From each side shoaling . . . The aggregated soil   X.288,293
Death with his mace petrific . . . smote and fixed . . .   X.294,295
And with asphaltic slime (broad as the gate,
Deep to the roots of hell) the gathered beach
They fastened, and the mole immense wrought on
Over the foaming deep high–arched, a bridge
Of length prodigious, joining to the wall
Immovable of this now fenceless world,
Forfeit to Death; from hence a passage broad,
Smooth, easy, inoffensive down to hell.   X.305

Adam's lament

O miserable of happy! Is this the end   X.720

Of this new glorious world, and me so late
The glory of that glory, who now become
Accursed of blessed! Hide me from the face
Of God, whom to behold was then my height
Of happiness! Yet well if here would end   X.725
The misery! I deserved it, and would bear
My own deservings. But this will not serve:
All that I eat or drink, or shall beget,
Is propagated curse. O voice, once heard
Delightfully, 'Increase and multiply,'   X.730
Now death to hear! For what can I increase
Or multiply, but curses on my head?
Who, of all ages to succeed, but feeling
The evil on him brought by me, will curse
My head? Ill fare our ancestor impure!
For this we may thank Adam! . . . So, besides   X.736,737
Mine own that bide upon me, all from me
Shall with a fierce reflux on me redound,
On me as on their centre . . . O fleeting joys   X.740,741
Of Paradise, dear bought with lasting woes!
Did I request thee, Maker, from my clay
To mould me man? Did I solicit thee
From darkness to promote me, or here place
In this delicious garden? As my will
Concurred not to my being, it were but right
And equal to reduce me to my dust,
Desirous to resign and render back
All I received, unable to perform   X.750
Thy terms too hard, by which I was to hold
The good I sought not. To the loss of that,
Sufficient penalty, why hast thou added
The sense of endless woes? Inexplicable
Thy justice seems. Yet to say truth, too late
I thus contest; then should have been refused
Those terms, whatever, when they were proposed.
Thou didst accept them: wilt thou enjoy the good,
Then cavil the conditions? And though God
Made thee without thy leave, what if thy son   X.760
Prove disobedient, and reproved, retort,
Wherefore didst thou beget me? I sought it not.

Wouldst thou admit for this contempt of thee
That proud excuse? Yet him not thy election,
But natural necessity, begot.
God made thee of choice his own, and of his own
To serve him; thy reward was of his grace,
Thy punishment then justly's at his will.   X.768
   Be't so, for I submit; his doom is fair,
That dust I am, and shall to dust return.
O welcome hour whenever! Why delays
His hand to execute what his decree
Fixed on this day? Why do I overlive,
Why am I mocked with death, and lengthened out
To deathless pain? How gladly would I meet   X.775
Mortality, my sentence, and be earth
Insensible! How glad would lay me down
As in my mother's lap! There I should rest
And sleep secure; his dreadful voice no more
Would thunder in my ears; no fear of worse   X.780
To me and to my offspring would torment me
With cruel expectation. Yet one doubt
Pursues me still, lest all I cannot die;
Lest that pure breath of life, the spi'rit of man
Which God inspired, cannot together perish
With this corporeal clod. Then, in the grave,
Or in some other dismal place, who knows
But I shall die a living death? . . . ['Tis so,]   X.788
That death is not one stroke, as I supposed,   X.809
Bereaving sense, but endless misery
From this day onward, which I feel begun
Both in me, and without me, and to last
To perpetuity. Ay me! that fear
Comes thund'ring back with dreadful revolution
On my defenceless head; both Death and I   X.815
Am found immortal, and incorporate[1] both.
Nor I on my part single, in me all
Posterity stands cursed. Fair patrimony
That I must leave you, sons! O were I able
To waste it all myself, and leave you none! . . .   X.820
[Thus Adam to himself lamented loud]   X.845
Through the still night, not now, as ere man fell,

Wholesome and cool and mild, but with black air
Accompanied, with damps and dreadful gloom,
Which to his evil conscience represented
All things with double terror. On the ground   X.850
Outstretched he lay, on the cold ground, and oft
Cursed his creation, death as oft accused
Of tardy[2] execution, since denounced
The day of his offence. Why comes not death,
Said he, with one thrice-acceptable stroke   X.856
To end me? Shall truth fail to keep her word,
Justice divine not hasten to be just?
But death comes not at call; justice divine
Mends not her slow pace for prayers or cries.
O woods, O fountains, hillocks, dales and bowers,
With other echo late I taught your shades
To answer and resound far other song . . .   X.862
                              O why did God,   X.888
Creator wise, that peopled highest heaven
With spirits masculine, create at last
This novelty on earth; this fair defect
Of nature, and not fill the world at once
With men as angels without feminineness?
Or find some other way to generate
Mankind? This mischief had not then befall'n,   X.895
And more that shall befall, innumerable
Disturbances on earth through female snares,
And strait conjunction with this sex. For either
He never shall find out fit mate, but such
As some misfortune brings him, or mistake;   X.900
Or whom he wishes most shall seldom gain
Through her perverseness, but shall see her gained
By a far worse, or if she love, withheld
By parents; or his happiest choice too late
Shall meet, already linked and wedlock-bound
To a fell adversary, his hate or shame . . .   X.906
     [Eve . . . proceeded in her plaint:]   X.909,913
     Forsake me not thus, Adam! Witness heaven
What love sincere, and reverence in my heart
I bear thee, and unweeting[3] have offended,
Unhappily deceived; thy suppliant

I beg, and clasp thy knees; bereave me not,
Whereon I live, thy gentle looks, thy aid,
Thy counsel in this uttermost distress, X.920
My only strength and stay. Forlorn[4] of thee,
Whither shall I betake me, where subsist?
While yet we live, scarce one short hour perhaps,
Between us two let there be peace, both joining,
As joined in injuries, one enmity
Against a foe by doom express assigned us,
That cruel Serpent. On me exercise not
Thy hatred for this misery befall'n,
On me already lost, me than thyself
More miserable; both have sinned, but thou X.930
Against God only; I against God and thee,
And to the place of judgment will return,
There with my cries importune heav'n, that all
Thy sentence from thy head removed may light
On me, sole cause to thee of all this woe,
Me, only me, just object of his ire. X.936
    She ended weeping, and her lowly plight,
Immovable till peace obtained from fault
Acknowledged and deplored, in Adam wrought
Commiseration; soon his heart relented X.940
Towards her, his life so late and sole delight,
Now at his feet submissive in distress,
Creature so fair his reconcilement seeking,
His counsel, whom she had displeased, his aid.
At once disarmed, his anger all he lost,
And thus with peaceful words upraised her soon . . . X.946
                              If prayers X.952
Could alter high decrees, I to that place
Would speed before thee, and be louder heard
That on my head all might be visited,
Thy frailty and infirmer sex forgiven,
To me committed and by me exposed. X.957
But rise, let us no more contend, nor blame
Each other, blamed enough elsewhere, but strive
In offices of love how we may lighten
Each other's burden in our share of woe.
Since this day's death denounced, if aught I see,

Will prove no sudden, but a slow-paced evil,
A long day's dying to augment our pain,
And to our seed (O hapless seed!) derived . . .   X.965
   Eve, thy contempt of life and pleasure seems   X.1013
To argue in thee something more sublime
And excellent than what thy mind contemns;
But self-destruction therefore sought refutes
That excellence thought in thee, and implies,
Not thy contempt, but anguish and regret
For loss of life and pleasure overloved.
Or if thou covet death, as utmost end   X.1020
Of misery, so thinking to evade
The penalty pronounced, doubt not but God
Hath wiselier armed his vengeful ire than so
To be forestalled; much more I fear lest death
So snatched will not exempt us from the pain
We are by doom to pay; rather such acts
Of contumacy[5] will provoke the Highest
To make death in us live . . .   X.1028
How much more, if we pray him, will his ear   X.1060
Be open, and his heart to pity incline,
And teach us further by what means to shun
Th'inclement seasons, rain, ice, hail and snow!
Which now the sky with various face begins
To show us in this mountain, while the winds
Blow moist and keen, shattering the graceful locks
Of these fair spreading trees; which bids us seek
Some better shroud, some better warmth to cherish
Our limbs benumbed, ere this diurnal star[6]
Leave cold the night.   X.1070

Notes on Book X

1. *Incorporate* – joined in one.
2. *Tardy* – slow.
3. *Unweeting* – ignorantly, undesignedly.
4. *Forlorn* – forsaken.
5. *Contumacy* – obstinacy.
6. *This diurnal star* – The sun; many suppose all the fixed stars are suns.

BOOK XI

The Argument

The Son of God presents to his Father the prayers of our first parents,
now repenting, and intercedes for them. God accepts them, but
declares that they must no longer abide in Paradise; sends Michael
with a band of cherubim to dispossess them; but first to reveal to
Adam future things. Michael's coming down. Adam shows to Eve
certain ominous signs; he discerns Michael's approach, goes out to
meet him. The angel denounces their departure. Eve's lamentation.
Adam pleads, but submits. The angel leads him up to a high hill, sets
before him in vision what shall happen till the flood.

Adam speaks to Eve

Eve, easily may faith admit, that all   XI.141
The good which we enjoy from heav'n descends;
But that from us aught should ascend to heaven
So prevalent as to concern the mind
Of God high-blest, or to incline his will,
Hard to belief may seem; yet this will prayer
Or one short sigh of human breath, upborne
Ev'n to the seat of God.   XI.148

Eve's lament

O unexpected stroke, worse than of death!   XI.268
Must I thus leave thee, Paradise? Thus leave
Thee, native soil, these happy walks and shades,
Fit haunt of gods; where I had hope to spend,
Quiet though sad, the respite of that day
That must be mortal to us both. O flowers,
That never will in other climate grow,
My earliest visitation and my last   XI.275

At ev'n, which I bred up with tender hand
From the first opening bud, and gave you names,
Who now shall rear you to the sun, or rank
Your tribes, and water from th'ambrosial fount?   XI.279
Thee lastly, nuptial bow'r, by me adorned
With what to sight or smell was sweet, from thee
How shall I part, and whither wander down
Into a lower world, to this obscure
And wild? How shall we breathe in other air
Less pure, accustomed to immortal fruits?   XI.285

   Adam replies to Michael

                And if by prayer   XI.307
Incessant I could hope to change the will
Of him who all things can, I could not cease
To weary him with my assiduous cries.
But pray'r against his absolute decree
No more avails than breath against the wind . . .   XI.312
Therefore to his great bidding I submit.   XI.314
This most afflicts me, that departing hence,
As from his face I shall be hid, deprived
His blessed count'nance; here I could frequent
With worship place by place where he vouchsafed
Presence divine, and to my sons relate,
On this mount he appeared, under this tree   XI.320
Stood visible, among these pines his voice
I heard, here with him at this fountain talked.
So many grateful altars I would rear
Of grassy turf, and pile up every stone
Of lustre from the brook, in memory[1]
Or monument[2] to ages, and thereon
Offer sweet-smelling gums and fruits and flowers.   XI.327
In yonder nether world where shall I seek
His bright appearances, or footsteps trace?
For though I fled him angry, yet recalled
To life prolonged and promised race, I now
Gladly behold though but his utmost skirts
Of glory, and far off his steps adore.   XI.333

Michael shows Adam a vision of Cain and Abel; Adam responds:

But have I now seen Death? Is this the way   XI.462
I must return to native dust? O sight
Of terror, foul and ugly to behold,
Horrid to think, how horrible to feel!
   To whom thus Michael: Death thou hast seen   XI.466
In his first shape on man; but many shapes
Of Death, and many are the ways that lead
To his grim cave, all dismal; yet to sense
More terrible at th'entrance than within.
Some, as thou saw'st, by violent stroke shall die,
By fire, flood, famine, by intemp'rance more
In meats and drinks, which on the earth shall bring
Diseases dire, of which a monstrous crew
Before thee shall appear; that thou mayst know   XI.475
What misery th'inabstinence of Eve
Shall bring on men. Immediately a place
Before his eyes appeared, sad, noisome, dark,
A lazar-house³ it seemed, wherein were laid
Numbers of all diseased, all maladies   XI.480
Of ghastly spasm, or racking torture, qualms
Of heart-sick agony, all feverous kinds,
Convulsions, epilepsies, fierce catarrhs,
Intestine stone and ulcer, colic pangs,
Demoniac frenzy⁴, moping melancholy,   XI.485
And moon-struck madness, pining atrophy⁵,
Marasmus, and wide-wasting pestilence,
Dropsies, and asthmas, and joint-racking rheums.
Dire was the tossing, deep the groans; Despair
Tended the sick, busiest from couch to couch;   XI.490
And over them triumphant Death his dart
Shook, but delayed to strike, though oft invoked
With vows, as their chief good, and final hope.
Sight so deform what heart of rock could long
Dry-eyed behold? Adam could not, but wept,
Though not of woman born; compassion quelled
His best of man, and gave him up to tears . . .   XI.497
   O miserable mankind, to what fall   XI.500
Degraded, to what wretched state reserved!

Better end here unborn. Why is life given
To be thus wrested from us? Rather why
Obtruded[6] on us thus? Who if we knew
What we receive, would either not accept
Life offered, or soon beg to lay it down,
Glad to be so dismissed in peace. Can thus
Th'image of God in man created once
So goodly and erect, though faulty since,
To such unsightly sufferings be debased   XI.510
Under inhuman pains? Why should not man,
Retaining still divine similitude
In part, from such deformities be free,
And for his Maker's image' sake exempt? . . .   XI.514
    There is, said Michael, if thou well observe   XI.530
The rule of not too much by temp'rance taught,
In what thou eat'st and drink'st, seeking from thence
Due nourishment, not gluttonous delight,
Till many years over thy head return.
So mayst thou live, till like ripe fruit thou drop
Into thy mother's lap, or be with ease
Gathered, not harshly plucked, for death mature.   XI.537
This is old age; but then thou must outlive
Thy youth, thy strength, thy beauty, which will change
To withered, weak, and grey; thy senses then
Obtuse,[7] all taste of pleasure must forego
To what thou hast; and for the air of youth,
Hopeful and cheerful, in thy blood will reign
A melancholy damp of cold and dry,
To weigh thy spirits down, and last consume
The balm of life. To whom our ancestor: XI.545
    Henceforth I fly not death, nor would prolong
Life much, bent rather how I may be quit,
Fairest and easiest, of this cumbrous charge,
Which I must keep till my appointed day   XI.550
Of rendering up, and patiently attend
My dissolution. Michael replied:
    Nor love thy life, nor hate; but what thou liv'st
Live well; how long or short permit to heaven . . .   XI.554
    To whom thus Adam, of short joy bereft: XI.628
O pity and shame, that they who to live well

Entered so fair, should turn aside, to tread
Paths indirect, or in the midway faint! . . .   XI.631

Michael shows Adam a vision of the flood and the ark

Meanwhile the south wind rose, and with black wings   XI.738
Wide-hovering, all the clouds together drove
From under heav'n . . . And now the thickened sky   XI.740,742
Like a dark ceiling stood; down rushed the rain
Impetuous, and continued till the earth
No more was seen; the floating vessel swum
Uplifted, and secure with beaked prow
Rode tilting o'er the waves; all dwellings else
Flood overwhelmed, and them with all their pomp
Deep under water rolled; sea covered sea,
Sea without shore; and in their palaces,   XI.750
Where luxury late reigned, sea-monsters whelped
And stabled; of mankind, so numerous late,
All left, in one small bottom swum embarked.
How didst thou grieve then, Adam, to behold
The end of all thy offspring, end so sad,   XI.755
Depopulation!⁸ Thee another flood,
Of tears and sorrow a flood thee also drowned,
And sunk thee as they sons; till gently reared
By th'angel, on thy feet thou stood'st at last,
Though comfortless, as when a father mourns
His children, all in view destroyed at once . . .   XI.761

Michael shows the destruction of Paradise

       Then shall this mount   XI.829
Of Paradise by might of waves be moved
Out of his place, pushed by the horned flood,⁹
With all his verdure spoiled, and trees adrift,
Down the great river to the opening gulf,¹⁰
And there take root, an island salt and bare,
The haunt of seals, and orcs,¹¹ and sea-mews' clang¹² . . .   XI.835

Adam rejoices in the promise of the rainbow

But say, what mean those coloured streaks in heaven,   IX.879
Distended as the brow of God appeased,
Or serve they as a flow'ry verge to bind

The fluid skirts of that same wat'ry cloud,
Lest it again dissolve and show'r the earth?   IX.883

Notes on Book XI

1. *In memory* – for myself.
2. *Or monument* – for my posterity.
3. *A lazar-house* – an hospital.
4. *Demoniac frenzy* – Those termed lunatics by one Evangelist are frequently termed *lunatics*, or possessed of the devil, by another.
5. *Atrophy* amd *marasmus* are a kind of consumption.
6. *Obtruded* – forced upon us.
7. *Obtuse* – blunted, dull.
8. *Depopulation* – dispeopling the earth.
9. *Pushed by the horned flood* – A river opposed in its course by an island or mountain, divides, and seems to push as with horns.
10. *To the opening gulf* – the sea opening wider and wider.
11. *Orcs* – a large kind of sea-fish.
12. *Clang* is properly the noise made by the flight of large flocks of birds.

BOOK XII

The Argument

The angel Michael continues from the flood to relate what shall succeed; then in the mention of Abraham comes by degrees to explain who that Seed of the woman shall be which was promised Adam and Eve in the Fall; his incarnation, death, resurrection, and ascension; the state of the church until his second coming. Adam, greatly satisfied and recomforted by these relations and promises, descends the hill with Michael; wakens Eve, who all the while had slept, but with gentle dreams composed to quietness of mind and submission. Michael in either hand leads them out of Paradise, the fiery sword moving behind them, and the cherubim taking their stations to guard the place.

Adam responds to Michael's prophesies

How soon hath thy prediction, seer blest,	XII.553
Measured this transient world, the race of time,	
Till time stand fixed! Beyond is all abyss,	
Eternity, whose end no eye can reach.	
Greatly instructed I shall hence depart,	
Greatly in peace of thought, and have my fill	
Of knowledge, what this vessel can contain;	
Beyond which was my folly to aspire.	XII.560
Henceforth I learn, that to obey is best,	
And love with fear the only God, to walk	
As in his presence; ever to observe	
His providence, and on him sole depend . . .	XII.564
[To whom thus also th'angel last replied:]	XII.574
This having learned, thou hast attained the sum	
Of wisdom; hope no higher, though all the stars	
Thou knew'st by name, and all th'ethereal pow'rs,	

All secrets of the deep, all nature's works,
Or works of God in heav'n, air, earth, or sea,
And all the riches of this world enjoy'st,   XII.580
And all the rule, one empire. Only add
Deeds to thy knowledge answerable; add faith;
Add virtue, patience, temperance; add love,
By name to come called charity, the soul
Of all the rest. Then wilt thou not be loath
To leave this Paradise, but shalt possess
A Paradise within thee happier far.   XII.587